EMPIRE

Classic Movie Scenes

André
Deutsch

First published in 1998 by
André Deutsch Ltd
76 Dean Street
London W1V 5HA
http://www.vci.co.uk

André Deutsch is a VCI plc company

A catalogue record for this book is available from the British Library.

ISBN 0 233 99601 X

Designed by WhiteLight
Printed and bound by Butler & Tanner, Frome and London

1 2 3 4 5 6 7 8 9 10

Contents

Introduction

WHAT MAKES a classic scene? What ingredients imbued in its script, direction and acting make it live on in history long after the film has been confined to TV schedules and rep houses? Well, if we all knew that we'd be millionaires by now, quaffing the finest champers on a pristine yacht drifting in the sunkissed Bahamas, only laying down anchor to return to LA to pick up an Oscar or call action on the next masterpiece. However, the magic of cinema is contained within those mysterious moments where everything fits and something truly great is created, be it for 30 seconds or 30 minutes.

They are not just about choice dialogue, although many of the following gems are built from the finest words ever to enter a screenplay. The scenes are also about what they envisage, the setting, the time, the one choice phrase that defined a moment in history. Take the Dr No classic, a card table, where most of the dialogue is the croupier's leadings in French, it takes just one final introduction to change cinema forever: "The name's Bond, James Bond." You can see it now, feel that tingle of expectation.

The classic scene page in Empire was designed to capture these moments in cinema. When the film title is spoken the first images that spring to mind are those fabled scenes. Mention On The Waterfront and you think of Brando's "Contender" speech; Reservoir Dogs the "Like A Virgin Debate"; Basic Instinct and it's the steamy interrogation of Sharon Stone's ice maiden Catherine Tramell. These are the scenes that have escaped the confines of their film to gain a life of their own. They are the stuff of endless Pub recollections, the punctuation points on our lives.

From It's A Wonderful Life to Heat, Bus Stop to LA Confidential, *Empire Classic Movie Scenes* covers all the majesty, humour, beauty, violence and joy of the movies. It'll make you want to return to those films, relive those moments, learn those lines to relay on demand and silence any debate. Read on…

Ian Nathan
Editor

"My Body Systems Will Slow Down – They Won't Stop..."

Bud and Lindsey, husband and wife from the undersea drilling rig, are facing certain death, stranded in the stricken submersible. It is rapidly filling with water and the pair have only one aqualung between them. Lindsey tries to persuade her husband to wear it, explaining that this is the only logical thing to do...

BUD: *(Shouting)* Fuck logic!

LINDSEY: Just listen to me for a minute. If you get this thing on and...You're a much better swimmer then I am, right?

BUD: Yeah, maybe...

LINDSEY: Right, yes. So I've got a plan...

BUD: What's the plan?

LINDSEY: I drown and you tow me back to the rig.

BUD: No...No!

LINDSEY: Yes, this water...

BUD: No!

LINDSEY:...Is a couple degrees above freezing, I go into deep hypothermia, my blood will go like ice water, my body systems will slow down – they *won't stop*...

BUD: *(Whispers)* Linds...

LINDSEY: ...You tow me back and I can be revived after maybe ten or 15 minutes.

BUD: *(Desperately)* Linds, put this on. You put it on...

LINDSEY: Ten or 15 minutes...

BUD: You put this on!

LINDSEY: No it's the only way, you just put this on, put this on, you know I'm right. *(Begging)* Please, it's the only way you've got, put this on. Bud please...

BUD: This is insane. *(He pauses, thinks*

FILM
The Abyss (1989)

DIRECTOR
James Cameron

STARRING
Ed Harris, Mary Elizabeth Mastrantonio, Michael Biehn

SCREENPLAY
James Cameron

OSCARS
Best Visual Effects

OSCAR NOMINATIONS
Best Cinematography, Best Art Direction, Best Sound

THE SCENE
Trying to rescue a nuclear submarine stranded on the seabed, the crew of an undersea drilling rig experience hallucinations which seem to be trying to communicate. The sub's Lieutenant Coffey (Biehn), driven insane, sets off in a minisub with a nuclear bomb. Bud (Harris) and Lindsey (Mastrantonio) give chase, but, after sending Coffey to a watery grave face one of their own...

about what she has been saying, then seems to make a decision) Okay, here, hold this.

LINDSEY: You can do this, you know…you can do this.

BUD: Oh God, Linds …(He is cut off before he can profess his love for his estranged wife, by the water in the submersible rising higher than nose level)

LINDSEY: I know, you can tell me later.

(They kiss passionately then Bud ducks beneath the water to put on the aqualung)

LINDSEY: Oh God! (Choking) Oh God, I'm scared…I can't breathe…I'm scared…

(The water fills the chamber. Lindsey grabs Bud's face mask and kisses him through it. He looks on in horror as his wife slowly drowns. Finally, as she dies, her hands go limp)

BUD: (Screams) NO!

7

Alfie

"What's It All About?..."

"'He's *younger* than you are.' That's what she said. Anybody'd think I was dodderin' about on bleedin' crutches…Trouble is, I still keep thinking about her. I can't get her out of me mind. Who'd have thought a ruddy great big lustbox like her would've found her way into anybody's feelings? She might have looked a hard case, but underneath she was quite mumsy, and she was in beautiful condition. Do you know, I'm beginning to think she was beautiful? After all, it ain't through the eyes that you see beauty, it's how the heart hungers for something that makes it beautiful.

(He's interrupted by another of his "birds", Siddie, having a brief exchange before returning his gaze into camera and continuing his train of thought)

You know what? When I look back on my little life and the birds I've known, and think of all the things they've done for me and the little things I've done for them, you'd think I'd had the best of it all along the line. But what have I got out of it? I got a bob or two, some decent clothes, a car. I got me health back, and I ain't attached. But I ain't got me *peace of mind*. And if you ain't got that, you ain't got nothing. I dunno. It seems to me if they ain't got you one way they got you another. So what's the answer? That's what I keep asking myself. What's it all about? Know what I mean?…"

FILM
Alfie (1966)

DIRECTOR
Lewis Gilbert

STARRING
Michael Caine, Vivien Merchant, Shirley Anne Field, Millicent Martin

WRITER
Bill Naughton (based on his play)

OSCAR NOMINATIONS
Best Picture, Best Actor (Michael Caine), Best Supporting Actress (Vivien Merchant), Best Screenplay, Best Song

THE SCENE
Alfie (Michael Caine) muses on life and love as he crosses Waterloo Bridge, talking to camera…

"You Still Don't Understand What You're Dealing With"

RIPLEY: Ash, can you hear me?

ASH: Yes, I can hear you.

RIPLEY: What was your special order?

ASH: You read it. I thought it was clear.

RIPLEY: What *was* it?

ASH: Bring back life-form. Priority one. All other priorities rescinded.

PARKER: Damn company. What about our lives, you son of a *bitch* ?

ASH: I repeat, all other priorities are rescinded.

RIPLEY: How do we kill it, Ash? There's gotta be a way of killing it – how, *how* do we do it?

ASH: You can't.

PARKER: That's *bullshit*...

ASH: You still don't understand what you're dealing with, do you? A perfect organism. Its structural perfection is matched only by its hostility.

LAMBERT: You *admire* it...

ASH: I admire its purity. A survivor. Unclouded by conscience, remorse, or delusions of morality...

PARKER: I've heard enough of this – I'm asking you to pull the plug.

ASH: I can't lie to you about your chances. But you have my sympathies...

FILM
Alien (1979)

DIRECTOR
Ridley Scott

STARRING
Tom Skerritt, Sigourney Weaver, John Hurt, Ian Holm, Veronica Cartwright, Harry Dean Stanton, Yaphet Kotto

WRITER
Dan O'Bannon, from a story by Dan O'Bannon and Ronald Shussett

OSCAR
Visual Effects

OSCAR NOMINATIONS
Art/Set Decoration

THE SCENE
The severed head of the android Ash (Ian Holm) is reactivated by Ripley (Sigourney Weaver), Parker (Yaphet Kotto) and Lambert (Veronica Cartwright), who desperately want to know how to kill the Alien at large aboard their ship, the Nostromo...

"Everyone Is In

(Bradlee opens his front door wearing pyjamas, a red checked dressing gown and a frown)

BRADLEE: *(Dryly)* Why the hell couldn't you tell me over the phone?

BERNSTEIN: Rumour says the phones aren't safe.

WOODWARD: Can't trust 'em.

BRADLEE: Come on in.

WOODWARD: We can't come in, sir.

BERNSTEIN: Rumour says there is electronic surveillance.

(Bradlee sighs and goes out with his journalists into his front garden)

BRADLEE: Surveillance? Who's doing it?

WOODWARD: It's being done. People's lives are in danger…

BRADLEE: Wait a minute…

WOODWARD: Maybe even ours.

BRADLEE: *(Turning to Bernstein)* What happened to that justice source of yours?

BERNSTEIN: I guess I made the instructions too complicated, because he thought I said, "Hang up", when I just said, "Hang on".

BRADLEE: Jesus.

WOODWARD: The story is right! Halderman was the fifth name to control that fund, and Sloan would have told a Grand Jury.

BRADLEE: Why didn't he?

WOODWARD: Nobody asked.

BERNSTEIN: Because nobody asked him.

WOODWARD: The cover-up had little to do with the break-in, it was to protect covert operations. There are covert activities involving the entire US intelligence community.

BRADLEE: Did Deep Throat say that people's lives are in danger? What else did he say?

FILM
All The President's Men (1976)

DIRECTOR
Alan J. Pakula

STARRING
Robert Redford, Dustin Hoffman, Jason Robards, Jack Warden, Hal Holbrook, Martin Balsam, Jane Alexander

SCREENPLAY
William Goldman

OSCARS
Best Supporting Actor (Jason Robards), Best Adapted Screenplay (William Goldman), Best Art Direction (George Jenkins, George Gaines), Best Sound (Arthur Piantadosi, Les Fresholtz, Dick Alexander, Jim Webb)

OSCARS NOMINATIONS
Best Picture (Walter Coblenz), Best Director (Alan J. Pakula), Best Supporting Actress (Jane Alexander), Best Editing (Robert L. Wolfe)

CLASSIC SCENE
Washington Post reporters Carl Bernstein (Hoffman) and Bob Woodward (Redford) have finally pieced together the shocking news, with the help of anonymous source Deep Throat (Holbrook), that the recent break-in at the Watergate building involves a plot of political corruption that goes all the way up to the White House and President Nixon himself. In fear of their lives and afraid they're being watched, they arrive late at the house of their editor Ben Bradlee (Robards) for the go-ahead to run the most controversial news story in US history…

volved..."

WOODWARD: He said that everyone is involved.

(Bradlee pauses and chews on the import of what he has just been told)

BRADLEE: You know the results of the latest Gallup poll? Half the country have never even heard the word Watergate. Nobody gives a shit. You're probably pretty tired, right? Well, you should be. Go home. Get a nice hot bath. Rest up. For 15 minutes. Then get your asses back in gear. We're under a lot of pressure here and you put us there. Nothing's riding on this except the first amendment of the constitution, the freedom of the press, and maybe the future of the country. Not that any of that matters. But if you guys fuck up, *I'm* going to get mad...

"Shut Up And Deal..."

MISS KUBELIK: Mr. Baxter! Mr. Baxter! Mr. Baxter! Mr. Baxter! *(She pounds on the door)*

(Baxter comes to the door holding a frothing bottle of champagne)

MISS KUBELIK: Oh. Are you all right?

BAXTER: *(Somewhat surprised)* I'm fine!

MISS KUBELIK: Are you sure? How's your knee?

BAXTER: I'm fine all over.

MISS KUBELIK: Oh. *(Sighs)* Would you mind if I come in?

BAXTER: Of course not.

(They go in and he shuts the door)

BAXTER: Let me get another glass.

MISS KUBELIK: *(Seeing that he's been packing)* Where are you going?

BAXTER: Oh, who knows...Another neighbourhood. Another town. Another job. I'm on my own.

MISS KUBELIK: That's funny, so am I. What did you do with the cards?

BAXTER: In there *(He points to one of the packing cases and she digs out a pack of playing cards. They sit on the sofa. He pours the champagne while she shuffles)*...What about Mr. Sheldrake?

MISS KUBELIK: We can send him a fruitcake every Christmas. *(She hands him the pack)* Cut. *(He takes one)*

BAXTER: I love you Miss Kubelik. *(She pretends not to hear him)*

MISS KUBELIK: Three...Queen.

BAXTER: Did you hear what I said, Miss Kubelik? I absolutely adore you. *(She continues to ignore him and takes his card back, shuffling it into the pack, which she then hands to him)*

MISS KUBELIK: Shut up and deal...

FILM
The Apartment (1960)

DIRECTOR
Billy Wilder

STARRING
Jack Lemmon, Shirley MacLaine, Fred MacMurray

SCREENPLAY
Billy Wilder and I.A.L. Diamond

OSCARS
Best Picture, Best Director, Best Original Screenplay, Best Editing, Best Art Direction

OSCAR NOMINATIONS
Best Actor (Jack Lemmon), Best Actress (Shirley MacLaine), Best Supporting Actor (Jack Kruschen), Best Cinematography (Black And White), Best Sound

THE SCENE
At a drunken New Year's Eve party, lowly elevator girl Fran Kubelik (MacLaine) suddenly realises that she's in love with kindly, lovelorn C. C. Baxter (Lemmon) and not her philandering boss, J.D. Sheldrake (MacMurray), with whom she's been having an affair As she races up the stairs of Baxter's apartment building, she hears what she thinks is a suicidal gunshot. The final scene of the film, it was hastily written 20 minutes before shooting and wrapped in one take...

"Smells Like...Victory."

"Smell that? Do you smell that?...Napalm, son. Nothing else in the world smells like that...*(He crouches down)* I love the smell of napalm in the morning. Do you know, one time we had a hill bombed. For 12 hours. When it was all over I walked up. We didn't find one of 'em, not one stinking dink body. But the smell...you know that gasoline smell? The whole hill...Smells like...Victory...*(A shell explodes behind him, but he doesn't flinch)*...Some day this war's gonna end..."

FILM
Apocalypse Now (1979)

DIRECTOR
Francis Ford Coppola

STARRING
Martin Sheen, Robert Duvall, Frederic Forrest, Marlon Brando, Sam Bottoms, Dennis Hopper

SCREENPLAY
John Milius, Francis Ford Coppola

OSCARS
Best Cinematography (Vittorio Storaro), Best Sound

THE SCENE
In the midst of Vietnam, against the billowing yellow smoke from an air strike, colourful Wagner fan Lieutenant Colonel Kilgore (Robert Duvall), resplendent in cavalry hat, enthuses to a stunned Captain Willard (Martin Sheen)...

"Games
Are
Fun…"

Basic Instinct

CORRELI: Would you tell us about the nature of your relationship with Mr. Boz?

CATHERINE: I had sex with him for about a year and a half...I liked having sex with him. He wasn't afraid of experimenting. I like men like that, men who give me pleasure. He gave me a lot of pleasure.

CORRELI: You ever, er, engage in any sado masochistic activity?

CATHERINE: *(Leans forward)* Exactly what did you have in mind Mr. Correli?

CORRELI: *(He licks his lips)* Ever tie him up?

CATHERINE: No.

NICK: You *never* tied him up?

CATHERINE: No. Johnny liked to use his hands too much...I like hands and fingers.

WALKER: You describe a white silk scarf in your book.

CATHERINE: I've always had a fondness for white silk scarves. They're good for all occasions.

NICK: But you said you liked men to use their hands didn't you?

CATHERINE: No, I said I liked *Johnny* to use his hands...I don't make any rules, Nick, I go with the flow.

CORRELI: Did you kill Mr. Boz, Miss Tramell?

CATHERINE: *(Takes off her jacket)* I'd have to be pretty stupid to write a book about killing and then kill somebody the way I described it in my book – I'd be announcing myself as the killer. I'm not stupid.

TALCOTT: We know you're not stupid Miss Tramell.

WALKER: Maybe that's what you're counting on to get you off the hook.

NICK: Writing the book gives you an alibi.

CATHERINE: Yes it does, doesn't it? The answer is no, I didn't kill him.

GUS: Do you use drugs Miss Tramell?

CATHERINE: Sometimes.

CORRELI: Did you ever use drugs with Mr. Boz?

CATHERINE: Sure.

GUS: What kind of drugs?

CATHERINE: Cocaine...Have you ever fucked on cocaine Nick? *(She uncrosses her legs)* It's nice.

NICK: *(Hot under the collar)* You like playing games, don't you?

CATHERINE: *(Playing with her lighter)* I have a degree in psychology, it goes with the turf...Games are fun.

FILM
Basic Instinct (1992)

DIRECTOR
Paul Verhoeven

STARRING
Michael Douglas, Sharon Stone, Jeanne Tripplehorn, George Dzundza

SCREENPLAY
Joe Eszterhas

OSCAR NOMINATIONS
Best Film Editing, Best Original Score

THE SCENE
Suspected of murdering retired rock and roller Johnny Boz, millionaire novelist Catherine Tramell (Sharon Stone) is brought in for questioning before a police panel – Assistant District Attorney Correli (Wayne Knight), Nick Curran (Michael Douglas), Lieutenant Walker (Denis Arndt), Gus (George Dzundza) and Captain Talcott (Chelcie Ross)...

"Did I Urinate On Your Rug?"

(A fat sixtyish man in a motorised wheelchair – Jeffrey Lebowski – enters the room where The Dude, wearing shorts and a bowling shirt, is sitting. Brandt, Mr Lebowski's assistant, withdraws)

LEBOWSKI: Okay, so, you're a Lebowski, I'm a Lebowski, that's teriffic. I'm very busy so what can I do for you?

DUDE: Well, sir, it's this rug I have, it really tied the room together...

LEBOWSKI: You told Brandt on the phone, he told me. So where do I fit in?

DUDE: Well they were looking for you, these two guys, they were trying to –

LEBOWSKI: I'll say it again all right? You told Brandt, he told me, I know what happened. Yes? Yes?

DUDE: So you know they were trying to piss on *your* rug –

LEBOWSKI: Did I urinate on your rug?

DUDE: You mean, did you personally come and pee on my –

LEBOWSKI: Hello! Do you speak English? *Parla usted Inglese?* I'll say it again. Did I urinate on your rug?

DUDE: Well, no, like I said, Woo peed on the rug –

LEBOWSKI: Hello! Hello! So every time – I just want to understand this, sir – every time a rug is micturated upon in this fair city, I have to compensate the –

DUDE: Come on, man, I'm

FILM
The Big Lebowski (1998)

DIRECTOR
Joel Coen

STARRING
Jeff Bridges, John Goodman, Julianne Moore, Steve Buscemi

SCREENPLAY
Ethan Coen and Joel Coen

THE SCENE
When slacker Jeffrey Lebowski (Bridges) – alias The Dude – is mistaken for another Lebowski (David Huddleston), a multi-millionaire businessman, his rug gets peed on by a pair of befuddled debt-collectors. Furious, The Dude meets his namesake and demands compensation...

---

not trying to scam anybody here, I'm just –

LEBOWSKI: You're just looking for a handout like every other – Are you employed, Mr Lebowski?

DUDE: Look, let me explain something. I'm not Mr Lebowski, you're Mr Lebowski. I'm The Dude. So that's what you call me, that, or Duder. His Dudeness. Or El Duderino, if, you know, you're not into the whole brevity thing –

LEBOWSKI: Are you employed, sir?

DUDE: Employed?

LEBOWSKI: You don't go out and make a living dressed like that in the middle of a weekday.

DUDE: Is this a – what day is this?

LEBOWSKI: But I *do* work, so if you don't mind –

DUDE: No, look. I do mind. The Dude minds...

(Having ordered drinks, Marlowe and Vivian, facing each other across a table, start discussing their extra-curricular habits)

VIVIAN: Tell me, what do you usually do when you're not working?

MARLOWE: I play the horses, fool around.

VIVIAN: No women?

MARLOWE: Oh, I'm generally working on something most of the time.

VIVIAN: Could that be stretched to include me?

MARLOWE: Oh, I like you, I told you that before.

VIVIAN: *(Her lips curling)* I like to hear you say it.

MARLOWE: Mmm...

VIVIAN: But you didn't do much about it.

MARLOWE: Well, neither did you.

"Depends On Who's In The Saddle..."

VIVIAN: Well, speaking of horses, I like to play them myself. But I like to see them work out a little first, see if they are frontrunners or come from behind. Find out what their whole card is, what makes them run.

MARLOWE: *(His brows lifting wryly)* Find out mine?

VIVIAN: *(Retrieving a cigarette from her bag)* I think so. I'd say you don't like to be rated, you like to get out in front, open up a lead, take a little breather in the back stretch and then come home free.

(Marlowe leans forward and lights her cigarette with a match)

MARLOWE: You don't like to be rated yourself.

VIVIAN: I haven't met anyone yet who could do it. Any suggestions?

MARLOWE: Well, I can't tell until I've seen you over a distance of ground. You've got a touch of class but I don't know how far you can go.

VIVIAN: A lot depends on who's in the saddle...

FILM
The Big Sleep (1946)

DIRECTOR
Howard Hawks

STARRING
Humphrey Bogart, Lauren Bacall, John Ridgely, Martha Vickers, Dorothy Malone

SCREENPLAY
William Faulkner, Leigh Brackett, Jules Furthman

THE SCENE
Having located – dead – the smutty-book dealer Geiger (Theodore Von Eltz), who was blackmailing his client General Sternwood (Charles Waldron) with compromising pictures of his daughter Carmen (Vickers) and covered up the fact that Carmen was drugged up at the scene of the crime, private investigator Philip Marlowe (Bogart) saunters into a bar to update the General's other daughter Vivian (Bacall). Here she surprisingly pays him off on a case that is still very much on-going, before distracting him with her innuendo soaked repartee. In return Marlowe gives as good as he gets and a scintillating sexual chemistry brews...

Blade Runner

FILM
Blade Runner (1982)

DIRECTOR
Ridley Scott

STARRING
Harrison Ford, Rutger Hauer, Sean Young, Daryl Hannah, Edward James Olmos, M. Emmet Walsh

SCREENPLAY
Hampton Fancher, David Peoples

OSCAR NOMINATIONS
Best Art Direction (Lawrence G. Paull), David L. Snyder (Art Direction), Linda DeScerina (Set Decoration), Best Visual Effects (Douglas Trumbull, Richard Yuricich, David Dryer)

THE SCENE
Los Angeles, 2019. With a group of replicants (android beings of super intelligence and human appearance) on the loose in LA after escaping from an off-world colony and arriving on Earth in an effort to lengthen their lifespans, it's down to blade runner, or android bounty hunter Rick Deckard (Harrison Ford) to retire them. However, just when things begin to look really bleak for Deckard during a rooftop confrontation with the seemingly indestructible android leader Roy Batty (Rutger Hauer), events take a rather unexpected turn…

"Time To Die…"

(Deckard is about to plunge from the rooftop he has been perilously hanging from, when Batty grasps his arm and pulls him to safety. As Deckard lies on the roof, breathless and astonished, Batty approaches him and kneels down near to where he is lying)

BATTY: *(In a slow, mournful voice)* I've seen things you people wouldn't believe. Attack ships on fire off the shoulder of Orion. I watched c-beams glitter in the dark near the Tanhauser Gate. All those …moments will be lost in time like tears in rain. *(He pauses)* Time to die…

(He smiles at the amazed Deckard, then hangs his head in sadness. As he does so a dove flies from his hand into the sky)

DECKARD: *(Voiceover)* I don't know why he saved my life. Maybe in those last moments he loved life more than he ever had done before. Not just his life. Anybody's life. My life. All he'd wanted were the same answers the rest of us want. Where do I come from? Where am I going? How long have I got? All I could do was sit there and watch him die…

"We Mustn't Behave Like This..."

ALEC: You know what's happened, don't you?

LAURA: Yes. Yes, I do.

ALEC: I've fallen in love with you.

LAURA: *(Sounding forlorn)* Yes, I know.

ALEC: Tell me honestly, please tell me honestly, if what I believe is true.

LAURA: What do you believe?

ALEC: That it's the same with you. That you've fallen in love too.

LAURA: It sounds so silly.

ALEC: Why?

LAURA: I know you so little.

FILM
Brief Encounter (1945)

DIRECTOR
David Lean

STARRING
Celia Johnson, Trevor Howard, Cyril Raymond, Stanley Holloway, Joyce Carey

SCREENPLAY
Anthony Havelock-Allan, David Lean, Ronald Neame

OSCAR NOMINATIONS
Celia Johnson (Best Actress), David Lean (Best Director), Anthony Havelock-Allan, David Lean, Ronald Neame (Best Original Screenplay)

THE SCENE
Housewife Laura Jesson (Johnson), whose Thursdays normally revolve around shopping trips to the nearby town of Milford Junction, suddenly finds her plans changed after a chance meeting with also married local doctor Alec Harvey (Howard) at the station cafe. Having spent two seemingly platonic afternoons together having lunch, going to the pictures and hiring a boat for a trip down the river, they stop off for a well-earned cuppa at the boatman's office, where Alec takes the opportunity to confess his true feelings...

ALEC: It is true though, isn't it?

LAURA: Yes, it's true.

ALEC: Laura

(Moves to touch her but she shrinks away)...

LAURA: No, please, we must be sensible, please help me to be sensible. We mustn't behave like this. We must forget that we've said what we've said.

ALEC: Not yet. Not quite yet.

LAURA: *(Anxiously)* But we must. Don't you see?

ALEC: *(Puts his teacup on the table, takes Laura's hands and looks into her eyes)* Listen. It's too late now to be as sensible as all that. It's too late to forget what we've said. And anyway, whether we've said it or not couldn't have mattered. We know. We've both of us known for a long time.

LAURA: How can you say that? I've only known you for four weeks. We only talked for the first time last Thursday week.

ALEC: Last Thursday week. Has it been a long time for you, since then? Answer me truly.

LAURA: Yes.

ALEC: How often did you decide that you were never going to see me again?

LAURA: Several times a day.

ALEC: *(Earnestly)* So did I.

LAURA: *(Laughs nervously)* Oh Alec –

ALEC: I love you. I love your wide eyes, the way you smile, and your shyness, and the way you laugh at my jokes.

LAURA: *(Protesting)* Please don't.

ALEC: I love you. I love you. You love me too. It's no use pretending it hasn't happened, because it has.

LAURA: Yes it has. I don't want to pretend anything either to you or to anyone else. But, from now on I shall have to. That's what's wrong, don't you see? That's what

spoils everything. That's why we must stop here and now talking like this. We're neither of us free to love each other – there's too much in the way. *(In a choking voice, on the verge of crying)* There's still time…if we control ourselves…and behave like sensible human beings…there's still time…to…

(Unable to hide her feelings any longer, she dissolves into tears and falls, weeping, into Alec's lap)

ALEC: *(Sadly, and with obvious despair)* There's no time at all…

FILM
Bringing Up Baby (1938)

STARRING
Katharine Hepburn, Cary Grant

SCREENPLAY
Dudley Nichols, Hagar Wilde from the story by Hagar Wilde

THE SCENE
In the definitive screen comedy, straight-laced zoologist David Huxley (Cary Grant) tries to halt the amorous, disaster-strewn attentions of madcap heiress Susan Vance (Katharine Hepburn). As they arrive home after a failed effort to see Mr. Peabody for a grant, David assures her that there really is nothing between them...

"I'm Strangely Drawn Toward You..."

DAVID: Now just a moment, Susan. Don't think that I don't appreciate all you've done, but, *(She tries to interject)*...just a *moment*, but there are limits to what a man can bear. Besides that, tomorrow afternoon I'm going to get married.

SUSAN: *(Giggling)*: What *for*?

DAVID: Well because, bec... well anyway, I'm going to get married, Susan, and don't interrupt. Now, my future wife has always regarded me as a man of some dignity *(She suppresses her giggles)*. Privately, I'm convinced that I *have* some dignity. Now it isn't that I don't *like* you, Susan, because,

after all, in moments of quiet I'm strangely drawn toward you. But, well, there haven't *been* any quiet moments. Our relationship has been a series of misadventures from beginning to end. So if you *don't* mind, I'll see Mr. Peabody *alone* and *unarmed*...

SUSAN: Without me?

DAVID: Yes, without you and *definitely* without you. Now, Susan, I'm going to say good *night*. And I hope that I never set eyes on you *again (He slams her car door)*. Good night. *(He wheels about, trips over the kerb and sprawls face-first on to the pavement...)*

"Well, What *Do* You Believe In Then?"

CRASH: I don't believe in quantum physics when it comes to matters of the heart.

ANNIE: Well, what do you believe in then?

CRASH: Well, I believe in the soul, the cock, the pussy, the small of a woman's back, the hanging curveball, high fibre, good Scotch, that the novels of Susan Sontag are self-indulgent, overrated crap. I believe Lee Harvey Oswald acted alone. I believe there ought to be a constitutional amendment outlawing astroturf and the designated hitter. I believe in the sweet spot, soft-core pornography, opening your presents Christmas morning rather than Christmas Eve, and I believe in long, slow, deep, soft, wet kisses that last three days. Good night.

FILM
Bull Durham (1988)

STARRING
Kevin Costner (Crash Davis), Susan Sarandon (Annie), Tim Robbins (Nuke LaLoosh)

SCREENPLAY/ DIRECTOR
Ron Shelton

THE SCENE
Baseball catcher Crash Davis (Costner) makes his classic speech to sophisticated team groupie Annie (Sarandon)...

"A Guy Who'll Be Sweet With Me…"

CHERIE: I don't know why I keep expecting myself to fall in love, but I do…I'm seriously beginnin' to wonder if there's a kind of love I have in mind…I don't know…Beau's the first one that ever wanted to *marry* me, since my cousin Malcolm. Naturally, I'd like to get married and have a family and all them things.

ALMA: But you've never been in love?

CHERIE: I don't know. Maybe I have and I didn't know it. That's what I mean. Maybe I don't know what love is. I want a guy I can looky up to, and admire. But I don't want him to *browbeat* me. I want a guy who'll be sweet with me. But I don't want him to baby me either! I just gotta feel that whoever I marry has some real regard for *me* – aside from all that lovin' stuff. You know what I mean?

FILM
Bus Stop (1956)

STARRING
Marilyn Monroe, Don Murray

DIRECTOR
Joshua Logan

SCREENPLAY
George Azelrod, adapted from the play by William Inge

OSCAR NOMINATIONS
Best Supporting Actor (Murray)

THE SCENE
Would-be chanteuse Cherie (Monroe), fleeing ardent cowboy Beau (Murray), wistfully explains to fellow traveller Alma (Hope Lang) the kind of man she's looking for…

Butch Cassidy And The Sundance Kid

BUTCH: Kid, the next time I say let's go some place like Bolivia, let's *go* some place like Bolivia.

SUNDANCE: Next time. Ready?

BUTCH: *(suddenly inspired)* No. We'll jump!

SUNDANCE: Like *hell* we will!

BUTCH: No, it'll be okay – if the water's deep enough 'n' we don't get squished to death. They'll *never* follow us.

SUNDANCE: How do *you* know?

BUTCH: Would you make a jump like that, you didn't have to ?

SUNDANCE: I *have* to and I'm not gonna.

BUTCH: But we got to. Otherwise we're dead. They're just gonna have to go back down the same way they come. Come on

SUNDANCE: Just one clear shot, that's all I want.

BUTCH: Come on.

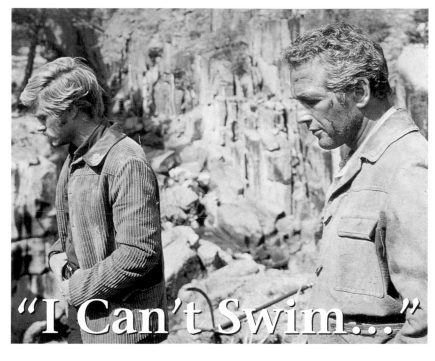

"I Can't Swim..."

SUNDANCE: Unh-uh.

BUTCH: We got to.

SUNDANCE: Nope! Get away from me.

BUTCH: Why?

SUNDANCE: *I wanna fight 'em!*

BUTCH: They'll kill us!

SUNDANCE: Maybe.

BUTCH: You wanna die?

SUNDANCE: DO you?

BUTCH: All right. *(unbuckling his gun-belt)* I'll jump first.

SUNDANCE: Nope.

BUTCH: Then *you* jump first.

SUNDANCE: *(hoarsely)* No I said.

BUTCH: What's a matter with you ?

SUNDANCE: *(yelling, embarrassed)* I CAN'T SWIM!

BUTCH: *(stares in disbelief, then laughs uproariously)* Why you *crazy* ? The *fall'll* probably kill ya!

SUNDANCE: Ohhhhhh...*(grabs the other end of Butch's gunbelt and they jump)* ohhh....shiiiiiiit!

FILM
Butch Cassidy And The Sundance Kid (1969)

DIRECTOR
George Roy Hill

WRITER
William Goldman

STARRING
Paul Newman and Robert Redford

OSCARS
Original Story and Screenplay (Goldman), Cinematography (Conrad Hall), Song (Bacharach-David), Original Score (Burt Bacharach)

OSCAR NOMINATIONS
Best Picture, Best Direction, Best Sound

THE SCENE
Pursued relentlessly by a superposse, Butch (Paul Newman) and Sundance (Robert Redford) have reached a dead end on a mountain path, cornered on a cliff edge. Far below is a stream. It seems there's only one way out...

"It's Never The Way You Expect It..."

The Crying Game

(At the flat, Dil sits in front of the dressing table mirror, while Fergus scans the flat and comes across a load of Jody's possessions)

DIL: What were you thinking of, hon'?

FERGUS: I'm thinking of your man.

DIL: Why?

FERGUS: I'm wondering why you keep his things?

DIL: *(Walking towards him)* I told you – I'm superstitious.

FERGUS: *(Moving in to stroke Dil's face)* Did he ever tell you you were beautiful?

DIL: *(In a hushed whisper)* All the time – even now.

FERGUS: What do you mean?

DIL: He looks after me. He's a gentleman.

(They move onto the net-curtain surrounded bed and begin kissing. Dil gets up off the bed)

DIL: Wait just one minute.

(Dil goes into the bathroom and comes back through the net curtains wearing a red robe. Fergus is taken aback)

FERGUS: *(Standing up)* Would he have minded?

(The pair kiss again and Dil's robe drops to the floor. A look of shock crosses Fergus' face and the camera pans down to reveal that Dil has a penis and is most definitely a man. Fergus, stunned beyond belief, releases his grasp and falls back on to the bed. Dil just stands, naked, in front of him)

DIL: You did know, didn't you?

FERGUS: *(Sitting on the bed, too shocked to speak)* Oh my God.

(Dil offers a hand but Fergus slaps it away and stands up)

FERGUS: Jesus, I feel sick.

DIL: Don't go, Jimmy.

(He slaps and knocks Dil to the floor in his rush for the bathroom)

DIL: I'm sorry, I thought you knew.

(Cut to: Fergus in the bathroom, vomiting into the sink. Dil, clad in robe once again, flounces onto the sofa and nervously lights a cigarette)

DIL: What were you doing in the bar if you didn't know?...I'm bleeding. It's all right Jimmy, I can take it – just not on the face. *(To himself)* You see I'm not a young thing any longer. Funny the way things go...(Aloud to Fergus) Don't you find that Jimmy? It's never the way you expect it...

(Fergus emerges from the bathroom)

FERGUS: *(Starting to leave)* I'm sorry.

DIL: You mean that? Don't go *(Dil falls to the floor and clings to Fergus' leg as he heads towards the door)* Jimmy – say something! Jesus...

FILM
The Crying Game (1992)

DIRECTOR
Neil Jordan

STARRING
Stephen Rea, Miranda Richardson, Forest Whitaker, Jim Broadbent, Jaye Davidson, Adrian Dunbar

SCREENPLAY
Neil Jordan

OSCARS
Best Screenplay

OSCAR NOMINATIONS
Best Picture, Best Director, Best Actor (Stephen Rea), Best Supporting Actor (Jaye Davidson), Best Editing

THE SCENE
Disillusioned IRA terrorist Fergus (Rea) has fled to London after taking part in the kidnapping of British soldier Jody (Whitaker), whom he befriended over one long night while holding him hostage, only for Jody to be accidentally killed in a desperate bid for freedom. Having escaped from terrorist colleagues Maguire (Dunbar) and Jude (Richardson), by heading for the capital, a guilt ridden Fergus meets with Jody's former lover Dil (Davidson), a hairdresser-cum-nightclub-singer who calls him Jimmy, and after a number of increasingly romantic rendezvous, the pair wind up back at her place...

RICK: Last night we said a great many things. You said I was to do the thinking for both of us. Well, I've done a lot of it since then and it all adds up to one thing. You're getting on that plane with Victor where you belong.

ILSA: But Richard, no, I, I…

RICK: Now you've got to listen to me. Do you have any idea what you'd have to look forward to if you stayed here? Nine chances out of ten we'd both wind up in a concentration camp. Isn't that true, Louis?

LOUIS: I'm afraid Major Strasser would insist.

ILSA: You're saying this only to make me go.

RICK: I'm saying it because it's true. Inside of us we both know you belong with Victor. You're part of his work. The thing that keeps him going. If that plane leaves the ground and you're not with him, you'll regret it.

ILSA: No…

RICK: Maybe not today, maybe not tomorrow, but soon, and for the rest of your life.

ILSA: What about us?

RICK: We'll always have Paris. We didn't have it, we'd lost it until you came

"Here's Looking At *You*, Kid…"

to Casablanca. We got it back last night.

ILSA: And I said I would never leave you.

RICK: And you never will. But I've got a job to do, too. Where I'm going, you can't follow. What I've got to do, you can't be any part of. Ilsa, I'm no good at being noble, but it doesn't take much to see that the problems of three little people don't amount to a hill o'beans in this crazy world. Someday you'll understand that. *(She begins to cry)* Now, now. Here's looking at *you*, kid…

FILM
Casablanca (1943)

STARRING
Humphrey Bogart, Ingrid Bergman, Paul Henreid, Claude Rains

SCREENPLAY
Julius J. Epstein, Philip G. Epstein and Howard Koch

DIRECTOR
Michael Curtis

OSCARS
Best Picture, Best Director, Best Screenplay

OSCAR NOMINATIONS
Best Actor (Bogart), Supporting Actor (Rains), Cinematography (Arthur Edeson), Film Editing (Owen Marks), Score (Max Steiner)

THE SCENE
Rick and Ilsa's parting at the airport must be the most famous farewell scene of the screen…

"Do I Feel Lucky?"

FILM
Dirty Harry (1971)

STARRING
Clint Eastwood as Inspector Harry Callahan

DIRECTOR
Don Siegel

SCREENPLAY
Harry Julian Fink, Rita M. Fink, Dean Riesner

THE SCENE
At the climax of the film, San Francisco Police Inspector 221 Harry Callahan, issues his famous challenge to the psychotic killer...

"Unh-uh! I know what you're thinking punk. You're thinking 'Did he fire six shots or only five?' Now, to tell you the truth I've forgotten myself in all this excitement. But being this is a .44 Magnum, the most powerful handgun in the world, and will blow your head clean off, you've gotta ask yourself a question...'Do I feel lucky?' Well, *do*...ya, punk?"

"Oh Captain, My Captain..."

(Mr. Nolan, the headmaster, has taken over the English class. A forbidding silence fills the room)

NOLAN: (Looking around) Alright then, we'll start over...What is poetry?

(No one answers. There's a knock at the door)

NOLAN: Come.

(Keating enters)

KEATING: Excuse me...I came for my

personals...Should I come back after class?

NOLAN: Get them now, Mr. Keating.

(Keating walks across the room. All the students' heads are bowed)

Dead Poets Society

NOLAN: Gentlemen, turn to page 21 of the introduction. Mr. Cameron read aloud the excellent essay by Dr. Pritchard on understanding poetry.

CAMERON: That page has been ripped out sir.

NOLAN: Well, borrow someone else's book.

CAMERON: They've all been ripped out, sir.

NOLAN: (Laughing incredulously) What do you mean they're all ripped out?

CAMERON: Sir, we...

NOLAN: Never mind. (Slams his book down in front of Cameron) Read!

CAMERON: Understanding Poetry by Doctor J. Evans Pritchard, Ph.D. To fully understand poetry.

(As Cameron continues to read the dry essay that Keating had previously derided and made his pupils tear from their books, Anderson looks up at his former teacher, who smiles sympathetically. Then, as Keating walks past, Anderson attempts to speak out about the clemency form that put the blame on the dismissed teacher)

ANDERSON: (Jumping up) Mr. Keating, they made everybody sign it.

KEATING: I know, Todd.

NOLAN: Quiet, Mr. Anderson!

ANDERSON: You've got to believe me!

KEATING: I do believe you, Todd.

NOLAN: Leave, Mr. Keating!

ANDERSON: (To Nolan) But it wasn't his fault!

NOLAN: Sit down, Mr. Anderson! One more outburst from you or anyone else and you're out of this school!

(Anderson sits down, exasperated)

NOLAN: Leave, Mr. Keating. I said leave, Mr. Keating!

(The class is silent as Keating begins to leave. Suddenly Anderson rises and climbs onto his desk top)

ANDERSON: Oh captain, my captain.

(Keating stops at the door and regards him)

NOLAN: (Furious) Sit down, Mr. Anderson Are you hearing me? Sit down. Sit down! This is your final warning, Mr. Anderson. How dare you?

(As Nolan confronts Anderson, other pupils get up on their desks and copy Anderson's lead, repeating: "Oh captain, my captain." Nolan furiously tries to regain control)

NOLAN: All of you, sit down. Leave, Mr. Keating!

(The boys ignore their headmaster and take one last look at their departing teacher)

KEATING: (His eyes filling with tears) Thank you, boys. Thank you...

FILM
Dead Poets Society (1989)

DIRECTOR
Peter Weir

STARRING
Robin Williams, Robert Sean Leonard, Ethan Hawke, Josh Charles, Gale Hansen, Kurtwood Smith, Norman Lloyd

SCREENPLAY
Tom Schulman

OSCARS
Best Original Screenplay

OSCAR NOMINATIONS
Best Picture, Best Actor (Robin Williams), Best Director (Peter Weir)

THE SCENE
Having inspired his pupils with his unorthodox teaching methods, English teacher John Keating (Williams), finds himself the scapegoat as a scandal rocks his public school: one of his finest students, Neil Perry (Leonard), shoots himself after a passionate disagreement with his legalistic father (Smith). Having been dismissed, Keating returns to the classroom for his personal items, to find Mr. Nolan (Lloyd), the headmaster, asking Cameron (Dylan Kussman) to read an essay the former teacher had previously ridiculed. Keating's presence, much to Nolan's consternation, inspires the pupils once more, and led by the shy Todd Anderson (Hawke), they stand on their desks and cry out a tribute to their beloved teacher with words of poetry he taught them...

"This Is This..."

STANLEY: Where the hell's my boots ? Anybody seen my boots? Somebody took my boots. I bought 'em special. All right you guys, whoever took my boots, I want 'em back.

AXEL: I gotta boot for you Stan, right up your ass.

(He kicks him.)

STANLEY: Hey Mike...Hey Mike, let me borrow your spares, huh? Your extra pair...

MIKE: No, Stan.

STANLEY: "No" ? Waddya mean, "No"?

MIKE: Just what I said, no...No means no.

STANLEY: Some fuckin friend. You're some *fuckin'* friend, you know that?

MIKE: You gotta learn, Stanley. Every time you come up here, you've got your goddamn head up your ass.

AXEL: Maybe he likes the view from up there!

(John laughs.)

MIKE: Every time he comes up he's got no knife, he's got no jacket, he's got no pants, he's got no boots. All he's got is that stupid gun he carries around, like John Wayne. *That* ain't gonna help you...

AXEL: Oh, what the hell, Mike. Give him the boots.

MIKE: No way. I'm not giving him no boots, no more...No more. No more. That's it.

STANLEY: You're a fuckin bastard. You know that, huh?

MIKE: Stanley, see this? This is *this*. This ain't something else...*This* is *this*. From now on, you're on your own.

STANLEY: *(Outraged)* I fixed you up a million times. *(To all of them)* I fixed him up a million times! I dunno how many times I must've fixed him up with girls. And nothing ever happens...zero. Hey, you know your trouble Mike, huh? No one ever knows

what the fuck you're talking about, huh?..."*This* is *this*" ? What the hell's that supposed to mean. "*This* is *this*"? I mean is that some faggot sounding bullshit, or is that some faggot sounding...

NICK: *(Cutting him off)* Shut up, Stan, will ya? Hey man, you're outta line.

MIKE: Watch out with that gun, Stanley. Watch out with the gun.

STANLEY: There's times...D'ya know what I think? You know what I think? There's times I swear I think you're a fuckin' faggot...

FILM
The Deer Hunter (1978)

DIRECTOR
Michael Cimino

STARRING
Robert DeNiro, John Savage, Christopher Walken, Meryl Streep, John Cazale

SCREENPLAY
Deric Washburn

OSCARS
Best Picture, Best Director, Best Supporting Actor (Christopher Walken), Best Sound, Best Editing

OSCAR NOMINATIONS
Best Actor (Robert DeNiro), Best Supporting Actress (Meryl Streep), Best Screenplay, Best Cinematography

THE SCENE
On a hunting jaunt in the mountains the day after Steven's (Savage) wedding, Stan (Cazale) reveals to Nick (Walken), John (George Dzundza) and Axel (Chuck Aspegren) that, not for the first time, he's come ill equipped for the conditions, petitioning Michael (De Niro) for his spare pair of boots. Michael takes the opportunity to give us his philosophy on life...

SHREVIE: Have you been playing my records?

BETH: Yes. So?

SHREVIE: So didn't I tell you about the procedure?

BETH: Yeah, you told me all about it, Shrevie. They have to be in alphabetical order.

SHREVIE: And what else?

BETH: *(Hesitantly)* Uh – they have to be filed alphabetically and according to year as well, okay?

SHREVIE: And what else? *(Beth begins to look a bit confused, and his temper takes a turn for the worse)* What else?

BETH: I don't know.

SHREVIE: You don't know. *(The record playing comes to a stop)* Well, let me give you a hint, okay? I found my James Brown record filed under the "J"s! Instead of the "B"s! I don't know who taught you to alphabetise! But to top it off, he's in the rock'n'roll section! Instead of the R&B section! How could you do that?!

BETH: It's too complicated, Shrevie. You see, every time I pull out a record there's this whole procedure I have to go through. *(Shrugs apologetically)* I just wanna hear the music, that's all.

"It's Just Music..."

SHREVIE: Is it too complicated to – just keep my records in the category, okay? Just put the rock'n'roll in with the rock'n'roll. Put the R&B in with the R&B. I mean, you're not gonna put Charlie Parker in with the rock'n'roll, would you ?

BETH: I dunno. Who's Charlie Parker?

SHREVIE: *(Looks at her exasperatedly, before shouting in disbelief)* Jazz! Jazz! He was the greatest jazz saxophone player that ever lived –

Miss Molly.

SHREVIE: Okay. Now ask me what's on the flip side.

BETH: What?

SHREVIE: *(Getting worked up once again)* Just – just ask me what's on the flip side, okay?

BETH: What is on the flip side?

SHREVIE: Hey Hey Hey Hey! 1958! Specialty Records! See? You don't ask me things like that, do you? No, you never ask me what's on the flip side!

BETH: No. Because I don't give a shit…

FILM
Diner (1982)

DIRECTOR
Barry Levinson

STARRING
Steve Guttenberg (Eddie), Daniel Stern (Shrevie), Mickey Rourke (Boogie), Kevin Bacon (Fenwick), Timothy Daly (Billy), Ellen Barkin (Beth)

OSCAR NOMINATION
Barry Levinson (Best Original Screenplay)

THE SCENE
Baltimore, 1959. Shrevie (Stern), one of six twentysomething college graduates who spend most of their spare time hanging out at the local diner, is beginning to feel that marriage to Beth (Barkin), isn't all it's cracked up to be, especially as he seems to have more fun with his mates than he does with his wife. The situation comes to a head one evening when Beth, ignorant of the differences between one type of music and another, drives Shrevie completely off his rocker by filing his treasured records in the wrong order…

BETH: *(Interrupting, trying to calm her irate husband)* Shrevie! What are you getting so crazy about? It's just music. It's not that big a deal.

SHREVIE: *(Still shouting)* It – it *is*! Don't you understand? This – this is important to me!

BETH: Shrevie, why do you yell at me? I never hear you yell at any of your friends.

SHREVIE: *(Picks up a handful of 45s and fans them out in front of Beth)* Look, pick a record, okay?

BETH: What?

SHREVIE: Just pick any record. Any record. *(Beth reluctantly chooses one)* Okay, what's the hit side?

BETH: *(Turning it over, seemingly unsure of which side is which)* Good Golly

Dr No

(The maître d'hôtel approaches the gaming table where the game is in progress)

SYLVIA: Suivi. *(She looks at her cards)*

CROUPIER: Suivi.

SYLVIA: Carte.

(The croupier passes her a card)

CROUPIER: Carte. Sept à la banque. Deux cents à la banque?

SYLVIA: Suivi.

CROUPIER: Banque au suivi? *(He passes her two cards)*

SYLVIA: *(Looking at her cards)* Carte.

CROUPIER: Carte.

(The man opposite her turns over his cards. They are an eight and a Jack. Sylvia looks at her cards: a five and a Queen. She loses)

CROUPIER: Huit à la banque.

SYLVIA: Suivi.

CROUPIER: C'est suivi.

FILM
Dr No (1962)

DIRECTOR
Terence Young

STARRING
Sean Connery, Ursula Andress, Joseph Wiseman, Jack Lord, Bernard Lee

SCREENPLAY
Richard Maibaum, Johanna Harwood, Berkely Mather

THE SCENE
After agent Strangeways has gone missing, presumed dead, in Jamaica, the British secret service sends an official to the Le Cercle Casino at Les Ambassadeurs in London to look for another of their agents, Commander James Bond, who is needed in Jamaica. Arriving at the casino, the official hands his card to the maître d'hôtel who we follow into the gaming room to a table where a game of chemin de fer is under way with the action focused on Sylvia Trench (Eunice Gayson) and a dark-haired man whose face we cannot see...

SYLVIA: *(To the croupier)* The house will cover the difference?

CROUPIER: Bien, Madame. Oui, Monsieur, changeur, s'il vous plaît.

(The mystery man deals two cards to Sylvia. And two for himself. She looks at her cards)

SYLVIA: Carte.

"Bond, James Bond..."

CROUPIER: Carte.

(The man turns over his cards. He has a nine and a King. He wins)

CROUPIER: Neuf à la banque.

SYLVIA: (To cashier) I need another thousand.

MAN: (Taking a cigarette from his case) I admire your courage, Miss, er...

SYLVIA: (Writing out a cheque) Trench. Sylvia Trench. I admire your luck, Mr...

(The camera finally rests on the man's face as he lights his cigarette)

MAN: Bond...James Bond...

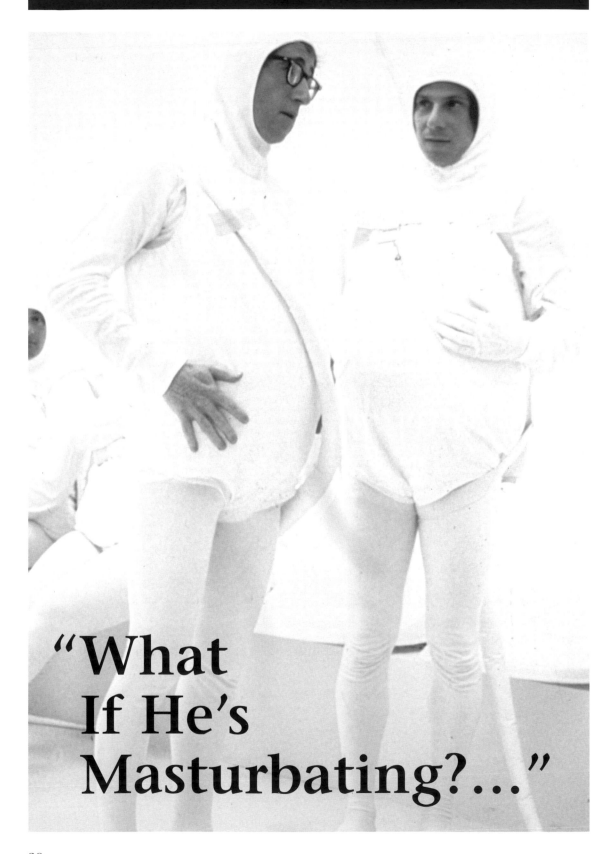

"What If He's Masturbating?..."

LEAD SPERM: Here we go again!

ALLEN SPERM: *(Panting with fear)* I'm not going out *there!* I'm not going to get shot out of that thing! What if he's masturbating? I'm liable to wind up on the ceiling! No...

THIRD SPERM: *(Attaching Allen sperm's rip-chord to the overhead static line)*: Get a grip on yourself.

ALLEN SPERM: *(Close to panic)*: Fellas, fellas! It's dark out there! I'm...I'm...I'm due at my parents for dinner.

(Cut to the penis engine room. Lots of burly men in white vests and silver safety helmets cranking machinery)

FOREMAN: Heave-ho! Heave-ho!

THE WORKERS: *(Singing)* Mine eyes have seen the coming of the glory of the lord...

(Cuts between: increasingly turned-on girl in car in parking lot seen through Sidney's eyes; penis engine room where the burly men continue to crank and sing; and Mission Control where the commander finally rises excitedly after peering into a submarine-style periscope)

COMMANDER: We're inside! We're making it! *(Paces away talking into a headset)* Have memory think of baseball players to keep sperms from premature launching.

(Cut back to sperms, the sound of a lone harmonica. The camera pans to reveal Allen playing it. Cut to brain)

SWITCHBOARD OPERATOR: *(Urgently, into red telephone)* We can't hold out any longer. Prepare for release of sperm.

COMMANDER: *(Pacing)* Willie Mays, Joe Nameth, Mickey Mantle...

(Cut to sperms, making their way up to the end of a long white corridor with the drone of aircraft engines in the background)

LEAD SPERM: *(Pausing at the opening)* See you guys in the ovary!

THIRD SPERM: Save me an egg!

ALLEN SPERM: *(Looking above and around him)* At least he's Jewish...

FILM
Everything You Always Wanted To Know About Sex (But Were Afraid To Ask) (1972)

DIRECTOR
Woody Allen

STARRING
Woody Allen, Lynn Redgrave, Anthony Quale, John Carradine, Lou Jacobi, Louise Lasser, Tony Randall, Burt Reynolds, Gene Wilder

SCREENPLAY
Woody Allen

THE SCENE
In the last of seven vignettes, Allen takes us inside the body of a man called Sidney where a host of tiny human beings staff each organ, directed from Mission Control – the brain – by commander (Oscar Beregi) and switchboard operator (Reynolds). During an impromptu "ball-her-right-there-in-the-parking-lot" encounter, the penis-cranking crew in the engine room are finally able to raise an erection after a rogue priest tampering with Sidney's guilt reflex has been arrested. En route from the gonads, the sperms (Allen, Robert Walden and a host of white clad extras) are poised two-by-two in the manner of marines about to parachute into enemy territory. Among them is Allen having second thoughts as Sidney prepares to try again...

"You Have To Ask Me Nicely..."

GALLOWAY: Do Code Reds still happen on this base, Colonel?

KAFFEE: Jo, the Colonel doesn't need to answer that.

GALLOWAY: Yes he does.

KAFFEE: No, he really doesn't.

GALLOWAY: Yeah, he really does...Colonel?

FILM
A Few Good Men (1992)

DIRECTOR
Rob Reiner

STARRING
Tom Cruise, Demi Moore, Jack Nicholson

SCREENPLAY
Aaron Sorkin (adapted from his own play)

OSCAR NOMINATIONS
Best Picture, Best Supporting Actor (Jack Nicholson), Best Editing, Best Sound

THE SCENE
Following the death of a young marine, Private Santiago, from an alleged piece of internal discipline – a "Code Red" – Navy lawyers Lt. Daniel Kaffee (Cruise) and Lt. Cmdr. JoAnne Galloway (Moore) are sent to question Santiago's commanding officer, Colonel Nathan R. Jessep (Nicholson) at Guantanamo Bay Naval Base, Cuba. The inexperienced Kaffee and Galloway are, however, meat and drink for the formidable Jessep, whom they first encounter having breakfast with his officer chums...

JESSEP: You know, it just hit me, she outranks you, Danny.

KAFFEE: Yes sir.

JESSEP: I wanna tell you something, and listen up 'cause I really mean this. You're the luckiest man in the world. There's nothing on this earth sexier, believe me gentlemen, than a woman you have to salute in the morning. Promote 'em all, I say, 'cause this is true. If you haven't gotten a blow job from a superior officer, well, you're just letting the best in life pass you by...

GALLOWAY: (Trying to remain calm) Colonel, the practice of Code Reds is still condoned by officers on this base, isn't it?

JESSEP: (Ignoring her question completely)... Of course, my problem is I'm a colonel, so I'll just have to go on taking cold showers until they elect some gal president.

(Jessep's officer cronies laugh)

GALLOWAY: I need an answer to my question, sir.

JESSEP: (Sternly) Take caution in your tone Commander, I'm a fair guy, but this fucking heat is making me absolutely crazy. You want to ask me about Code Reds. On the record, I tell you I discourage the practice in accordance with the commanders' directive. Off the record, it is an invaluable part of close infantry training, and if it happens to go on without my knowledge, so be it. I run my unit how I run my unit. You want to investigate me? Roll the dice and take your chances. I eat my breakfast 300 yards from 4,000 Cubans who are trained to kill me, so don't for one second think that you can come down here, flash your badge and make me nervous (He puffs on a cigar).

KAFFEE: (To Galloway) Let's go.

(They get up to leave. Kaffee turns back)

KAFFEE: (Gingerly) Colonel, I just need a copy of Santiago's transfer order.

JESSEP: What's that?

KAFFEE: Santiago's transfer order. You guys have paperwork on that kind of thing. I just need it for the file.

JESSEP: For the file?

KAFFEE: Yeah.

JESSEP: *(Condescendingly)* Of course you can have a copy of the transfer order for the file, Danny. I'm here to help in any way I can.

KAFFEE: Thank you.

JESSEP: You believe that, don't you Danny? That I'm here to help you in an way I can.

KAFFEE: Of course.

JESSEP: The corporal will take you by personnel on your way out to the flight line and you can have all the transfer orders that you want.

KAFFEE: Let's go.

JESSEP: But you have to ask me nicely.

KAFFEE: I beg your pardon?

JESSEP: You have to ask me nicely...You see, Danny, I can deal with the bullets and the bombs and the blood. I don't want money and I don't want medals. What I do want is for you to stand there in that faggoty white uniform and, with your Harvard mouth, extend me some *fucking courtesy*...You gotta ask me *nicely*.

KAFFEE: *(Rattled)* Colonel Jessep, if it's not too much trouble I'd like a copy of the transfer order...*Sir*.

JESSEP: *(Grinning triumphantly)* No problem.

A Fistful Of Dollars

(The Man With No Name walks back along the main street of the town, eyeing his quarry while chewing a cheroot. He passes the undertaker's shop, where the bearded old carpenter is buffing wood and humming to himself)

NO NAME: *(To undertaker)* Get three coffins ready…

UNDERTAKER: Er, uh.

(The undertaker looks on bemused as No Name strolls on through the town to the corral where Baxter's gang of gunslingers are attending their horses)

FIRST GUNSLINGER: *Adios amigo.* Listen stranger, you get the idea? We don't like to see bad boys like you in town. Go get your mule. You let him get away from you. *(Laughs mockingly)*

NO NAME: You see, that's what I want to talk to you about. He's feeling real bad.

FIRST GUNSLINGER: Uh?

NO NAME: My mule. You see, he got all riled up when you men fired those shots at his feet.

(Baxter's men glance at each other suspiciously)

SECOND GUNSLINGER: Hey, you making some kind of joke?

NO NAME: No. No. You see, I understand you men

FILM
A Fistful Of Dollars (1964)
DIRECTOR
Sergio Leone
STARRING
Clint Eastwood (The Man With No Name), Marianne Koch (Marisol), Wolfgang Lukschy (John Baxter), Gian Maria Volonte (Ramon Rojo)
SCREENPLAY
Sergio Leone, Duccio Tessari
THE SCENE
Having ridden into an unnamed small town on a rather sorry looking mule, the Man With No Name (Eastwood) is somewhat disgruntled when his animal is attacked by a gang of gunslingers working for town sheriff John Baxter (Lukschy), head of one of the families involved in a bitter power struggle for control of the town. Despite repeated warnings to leave the town, our poncho-ed hero merely grits his teeth and returns to avenge himself on his would-be assailants…

were just playing around, but the mule, he just doesn't get it. Of course, if you were to all apologise…

(Baxter's men stare at him in disbelief, before laughing in derision)

NO NAME: *(Threateningly)* I don't think it's nice, you laughing. You see, my mule don't like people laughing. He gets the crazy idea you're laughing at him. Now if you apologise, like I know you're going to, I might convince him that you really didn't mean it.

(There is a long silence as everybody stares at everybody else. It's broken by the second gunslinger, who spits meaningfully and reaches for his gun. But, before he can, No Name draws and shoots all four of them dead in a second, before twirling his

gun back into his holster. The sheriff, John Baxter, then appears)*

BAXTER: I saw the whole thing, you killed all four of them. You'll pay all right,

"Get Three Coffins Ready..."

you'll be strung up.

NO NAME: (*Reaches for his gun again*) Who are you?

BAXTER: Don't fire a shot.

I'm John Baxter...sheriff.

NO NAME: Yeah, well, if you're sheriff, you better get these men underground.

(*He turns and heads back the way he came. Passing the undertaker's shop, he speaks again to the old man*) My mistake. Four coffins...

Fatal Attraction

"You're Scared Of Me, Aren't You?…"

FILM
Fatal Attraction (1987)

DIRECTOR
Adrian Lyne

STARRING
Michael Douglas,
Glenn Close, Anne Archer

WRITER
James Dearden

OSCAR NOMINATIONS
Picture, Direction, Actress
(Close), Supporting Actress
(Archer), Adapted
Screenplay (Dearden),
Film Editing

THE SCENE
Spurned mistress Alex
Forrest (Glenn Close)
delivers her chilling
message via tape to
married philanderer Dan
Gallagher (Michael
Douglas)…

"Hello, Dan. Are you surprised? This is what you've reduced me to. I guess you thought you'd get away with it. Well, you can't…because part of you is growing inside of me and that's a fact, Dan, and you'd better start learning how to deal with it. Yes, you know I…I feel you. I *taste* you. I…*think* you. I *touch* you. Can you understand? *Can* you? I'm just asking you to acknowledge your responsibilities. (*Laughs*) Is that so bad? I don't think so. I don't think it's unreasonable. And, you know, another thing is that you thought that you could just walk into my life and turn it upside down without a thought for anyone but yourself…You know what you are, Dan? You're a cocksucking son of a bitch. I hate you. I bet you don't even *like* girls, do you ? Hah! You flaming fucking faggot. We probably *scare* you. Well, I know *I* do. You're scared of me, aren't you? You are. You're frightened of me, you're afraid. You're fucking afraid, aren't you? Why, you gutless, heartless, spineless fucking son of a bitch…I *hate* you. You deserve *everything* you get…"

Five Easy Pieces

"Hold the Chicken..."

BOBBY: I'd like a plain omelette, no potatoes, tomatoes instead, a cup of coffee and wheat toast.

WAITRESS: No substitutions.

BOBBY: What do you mean? You don't have any tomatoes?

WAITRESS: Only what's on the menu. You can have a Number Two. A plain omelette. It comes with cottage fries and rolls.

BOBBY: Naw, I know what it comes with, but it's not what I want.

WAITRESS: Well, I'll come back when you make up your mind.

BOBBY: Wait a minute, I have made up my mind. I'd like a plain omelette, no potatoes on the plate, a cup of coffee and a side order of wheat toast.

WAITRESS: I'm sorry, we don't have any side orders of toast. I'll give you an English muffin or a coffee roll.

BOBBY: What do you mean you don't make side orders of toast? You make sandwiches, don't you ?

WAITRESS: Would you like to talk to the manager?

BOBBY: You've got bread? And a toaster of some kind?

WAITRESS: I don't make the rules.

BOBBY: Okay, I'll make it as easy for you as can. I'd like an omelette. Plain. And chicken salad sandwich on wheat toast. No mayonnaise, no butter, no lettuce. And a cup of coffee.

WAITRESS: A Number Two.

Chicken sal san. Hold the butter, the lettuce and the mayonnaise. And a cup of coffee.

BOBBY: Yeah. Now all you have to do is hold the chicken, bring me the toast, give me a check for the chicken salad sandwich and you haven't broken any rules.

WAITRESS: You want me to hold the chicken, huh?

BOBBY: I want you to hold it between your knees.

WAITRESS: You see that sign sir? Yes, y'all have leave. I'm not taking any more of your smartness and sarcasm.

(Bobby puts on his sunglasses)

BOBBY: You see this sign?

(He violently swipes everything off the table)

FILM
Five Easy Pieces (1970)

STARRING
Jack Nicholson as Robert Eroica Dupea

WRITER
Adrien Joyce

DIRECTOR
Bob Rafelson

OSCAR NOMINATIONS
Best Picture, Best Actor, Best Supporting Actress (Karen Black), Best Story and Screenplay

THE SCENE
Bobby Dupea has rejected a cultured background and musical career to drift aimlessly, but he agrees to return home to see his invalid father. En route Bobby, girlfriend Rayette and two cranky hitchhikers stop for breakfast at a coffee shop, where Bobby not unreasonably wants some toast...

"Have You Ever Heard Of Insect Politics?..."

(Brundlefly stares accusingly at himself in a bathroom cabinet mirror)

BRUNDLEFLY:
You're a relic, yes you are. Vestigial, archaeological, redundant...*(He opens the cabinet, inside which are other parts of his body including an ear and penis, and places the tooth along with them)*...artefacts of a bygone era, of historical interest only.

(Behind him Veronica enters. Brundlefly catches sight of her in the mirror and turns to meet her)

BRUNDLEFLY:
You've missed some good moments. Is that why you're here, to catch up?

VERONICA:
(Horrified and full of pity at his terrifying appearance) I wanted...

BRUNDLEFLY: My teeth have begun to fall out. My medicine cabinet is now the Brundle Museum Of Natural History. Want to see what else is in it? *(She shakes her head)* Then what do you want?

VERONICA: *(Trying to control herself)* I came to tell you...I, um, just wanted to see you before...

BRUNDLEFLY: You have to leave now, and never come back here... *(His mind wanders)* Have you ever heard of insect politics? *(She shakes her head)* Neither have I. Insects don't have politics. They're very brutal. No compassion, no compromise. We can't trust the insect. *(He thinks aloud)* I'd like to become the first insect politician. See I'd like to but...I'm afraid.

VERONICA:
(Beginning to weep) I don't know what you're trying to say...

BRUNDLEFLY: I'm saying... *(He moves towards her and she backs away, unable to help herself)* I'm saying I'm an insect who dreamt he was a man, and loved it, but now the dream is over and the insect is awake.

VERONICA: No Seth...

BRUNDLEFLY: I'm saying...I'll hurt you if you stay.

(Veronica runs from the building in tears. Behind her Brundlefly holds his head in his hands shuddering and making half human sobbing sounds)

FILM
The Fly (1986)

DIRECTOR
David Cronenberg

STARRING
Jeff Goldblum, Geena Davis, John Getz

SCREENPLAY
Charles Edward Pogue, David Cronenberg

OSCARS
Best Make-up (Chris Wales, and Stephen Dupuis)

THE SCENE
Unorthodox but brilliant scientist Seth Brundle (Goldblum) has been experimenting with his research project – a new teleportation device. During the first human test, which he carries out on himself, a housefly flies into one of the pods. This results in the genetic splicing of himself and the fly, leading to the creation of "Brundlefly", a rapidly mutating monster. Later, girlfriend Veronica (Davis) discovers that she is pregnant by Brundle but resists her desire for an abortion, instead persuading ex-boyfriend Stathis (Getz) to take her to Brundle's lab to confront him. Inside, Brundlefly is dealing with the fact that his teeth have begun to fall out...

"You've Got To Come Back A Star!…"

FILM
42nd Street (1933)

DIRECTORS
Lloyd Bacon, Busby Berkeley

STARRING
Warner Baxter, Ruby Keeler, Dick Powell, Bebe Daniels, Guy Kibbee, Ginger Rogers

SCREENPLAY
Rian James and James Seymour. Based on the novel by Bradford Ropes

THE SCENE
Chorus girl Peggy Sawyer (Keeler in her film debut) has to replace her show's injured leading lady on opening night. In the wings frantic director Julian Marsh (Baxter) gives her the most famous pep talk in motion pictures…

"Sawyer, you listen to me, and you listen hard. Two hundred people, 200 jobs, $200,000, five weeks of *grind* and blood and sweat depend upon you. It's the lives of all these people who've worked with you. You've got to go on and you have to *give* and *give* and *give*. They've *got* to like you. *Got* to, do you understand? You *can't* fall down. You *can't*, because your future's in it, my future and everything all of us have is staked on you. All right, now I'm through. But you keep your feet on the ground and your head on those shoulders of yours and go out. And Sawyer, you're going out a *youngster*, but you've got to come back a *star*!…"

"Let Me See Your War Face..."

JOKER: *(Shouting)* Sir, I said it, sir!

HARTMAN: *(Shouting louder)* Well, no shit. What've we got here, a fucking comedian? Private

Joker, I admire your honesty. Hell, I like you. You can come over to my house and fuck my sister! *(Hartman punches Joker in the stomach. He falls gasping to the ground)*

HARTMAN: You little scumbag! I got your name...I got your ass! You will not laugh, you will not cry, you will learn by the numbers – I will teach you. Now get up, get on your

Full Metal Jacket

JOKER: Sir, to kill, sir!

HARTMAN: So you're a killer?

JOKER: Sir, yes, sir!

HARTMAN: Let me see your war face...

JOKER: Sir?

HARTMAN: You got a war face? *(Hartman demonstrates by pulling a terrifying "about-to-kill" expression and bellows in Joker's face)* Aaaaaaaaaaaggghhhh! That's the war face...

JOKER: *(Doing his best to copy Hartman's example)* Aaaaaagggghhh!

HARTMAN: Bullshit! You didn't convince me. Lemme see your real war face.

JOKER: *(Screaming)* Aaaaaaaaaggghhh!

HARTMAN: You don't scare me. Work on it.

JOKER: Sir, yes, sir!

(Hartman moves along the line of bunks to the next recruit)

HARTMAN: What's your excuse?

COWBOY: Sir, excuse for what, sir?

HARTMAN: *(Incensed)* I'm asking the fucking questions here Private. Do you understand?

COWBOY: Sir, yes, sir!

HARTMAN: Well thank-you-very-much, can I be in charge for a while?

COWBOY: Sir, yes, sir!

HARTMAN: Are you shook up? Are you nervous?

COWBOY: Sir, I am, sir!

HARTMAN: Do I make you nervous?

COWBOY: *(Hesitating)* Sir...

HARTMAN: Sir what? Were you about to call me an asshole?...

feet. You had best unfuck yourself or I will unscrew your head and shit down your neck.

JOKER: Sir, yes, sir!

HARTMAN: Private Joker, why did you join my beloved corps?

FILM
Full Metal Jacket (1987)

DIRECTOR
Stanley Kubrick

STARRING
Matthew Modine, Adam Baldwin, Vincent D'Onofrio, Lee Ermey, Dorian Harewood, Arliss Howard

SCREENPLAY
Stanley Kubrick, Michael Herr, Gustav Hasford (Based on the novel The Short Timers by Gustav Hasford)

OSCAR NOMINATION
Stanley Kubrick, Michael Herr, Gustav Hasford (Best Adapted Screenplay)

THE SCENE
In preparation to their new army life and later for service in Vietnam, a gaggle of terrified new recruits line up beside their beds in a stark bunkhouse to meet the drill instructor Gunnery Sergeant Hartman (Ermey) with whom they will share the next few weeks of their lives. After laying down the law in no uncertain terms he rounds on one recruit he has re-christened Pvt. Cowboy (Howard) who he suspects has dared to impersonate John Wayne without being spoken to. And forgot to say "sir" first and last. Then Pvt. Joker (Modine) owns up...

Glengarry Glen Ross

"I'm Here On A Mission Of Mercy"

BLAKE: *(To Williamson)* Are they all here?

WILLIAMSON: All but one.

BLAKE: Well, I'm going anyway. Let's talk about something important. *(He looks up at Levine about to pour himself a coffee)* Put that coffee down! Coffee's for closers only. *(Levine laughs then flinches as Blake turns to him)* You think I'm fucking with you? I am not fucking with you. I'm here from downtown. I'm here from Mitch and Murray. And I'm here on a mission of mercy. *(Looks at Levine again)* Your name's Levine?

LEVINE: Yeah.

BLAKE: You call yourself a salesman you son of a bitch?

MOSS: I ain't gotta listen to this shit.

BLAKE: *(To Moss)* You certainly don't, pal, because the good news is you're fired. The *bad* news is you've got – *all* of you've got just one week to regain your jobs starting with tonight. Starting with tonight's sits...Oh, have I got your attention now?

Good. Because we're adding a little something to this month's sales contest. As you all know, first prize is a Cadillac Eldorado. Anybody wanna see second prize? *(He raises second prize)*

Second prize is a set of steak knives. Third prize is you're fired. You get the picture? You laughing now? You got leads. Mitch and Murray paid good money... get their names to sell

50

them. You can't close the leads you're given. You can't close shit. You *are* shit! Hit the bricks pal, and beat it, 'cause you are going out.

LEVINE: The leads are weak.

BLAKE: The leads are weak? The fucking leads are weak? *You* are weak. I've been in this business 15 years.

MOSS: What's your name?

BLAKE: *Fuck you.* That's my name. You know why, mister? Cause you drove a Hyundai to get here tonight, I drove an $80,000 BMW. That's my name. *(To Levine)* And your name is "You're wanting" and you can't play in the man's game. You can't close them? Then go home, and tell your wife your troubles. Because only one thing counts in this life – get

them to sign on the line which is dotted. You hear me, you fucking faggots? *(Walks over to a blackboard and flips it over to reveal some letters)* ABC. A – Always. B – Be. C – Closing. Always Be Closing. Always *be closing.* AIDA – Attention, Interest, Decision, Action. Attention – do I have your attention? Interest – are you interested? I know you are because it's fuck or walk. You close or you hit the bricks. Decision – have you made your decision for Christ? And Action. AIDA - get out there. You've got the prospects coming in. You think they came in to get out of the rain? A guy don't walk on the lot unless he wants to buy. They are sitting out there, waiting to give you their money. Are you going to take it? Are you man enough to take it?...

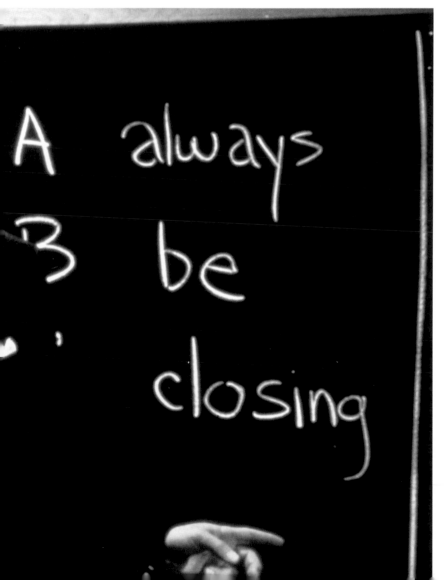

FILM
Glengarry Glen Ross (1992)

DIRECTOR
James Foley

STARRING
Al Pacino, Jack Lemmon, Alec Baldwin, Ed Harris, Alan Arkin, Kevin Spacey, Jonathan Pryce

SCREENPLAY
David Mamet

OSCAR NOMINATIONS
Best Supporting Actor (Al Pacino)

THE SCENE
It's 7.30 pm and in the offices of real estate agency Premiere Properties salesmen Shelley "The Machine" Levine (Jack Lemmon), Dave Moss (Ed Harris) and George Aaronow (Alan Arkin) have an impromtu meeting with their boss John Williamson (Kevin Spacey). Everybody but the cocksure Ricky Roma (Al Pacino) is present to hear company man Blake's (Alec Baldwin) pep talk...

"You're My Older Brother, And I Love You..."

MOE: *(Striding into Michael's hotel room, bubbling with bonhomie)* Hey Mike! Hello fellas, everybody's here. Freddie, Tom. Good to see you, Mike.

MICHAEL: How are you Moe?

MOE: All right. You got everything you want? The chef cooked for you special, the dancers will kick your tongue out and your credit is good. *(To Fredo)* Draw chips for everybody in the room so they can play on the house. *(He pulls up a chair, facing Michael across the table)*

MICHAEL: Well...my credit good enough to buy you out?

(Fredo sniggers in disbelief)

MOE: Buy me out?

MICHAEL: The casino. The hotel. The Corleone family wants to buy you out.

MOE: *(Suddenly losing his rag)* The Corleone family wants to buy me out? No. I buy you out, you don't buy me out.

MICHAEL: *(Entirely unflustered)* Your casino loses money. Maybe we can do better.

MOE: You think I'm skimming off the top, Mike?

MICHAEL: *(Shrugs)* You're unlucky.

MOE: *(Stands up)* You goddamn guineas really make me laugh! I do you a favour and take Freddie in when you're having a bad time and then you try to push me out!

(Fredo looks distinctly embarrassed)

MICHAEL: Wait a minute. You took Freddie in because the Corleone family bankrolled your casino because the Molinard family on the coast guaranteed his safety. Now we're talking business – let's talk business.

MOE: *(Sits back down at the table)* Yes, let's talk business, Mike. First of all, you're all done. The Corleone family don't even have that kind of muscle any more. The Godfather is sick, right? You're getting chased out of New York by Barzini and the other families. What do you think is going on here? You think you can come to my hotel and take over? I talked to Barzini. I can make a deal with him and still keep my hotel. *(He bangs the table, rattling the crockery)*

MICHAEL: *(Utterly*

FILM
The Godfather (1972)

DIRECTOR
Francis Ford Coppola

STARRING
Marlon Brando, Al Pacino, James Caan, Richard Castellana, Robert Duvall, Sterling Hayden, Diane Keaton

SCREENPLAY
Mario Puzo, Francis Ford Coppola

OSCARS
Best Picture, Best Actor (Marlon Brando), Best Adapted Screenplay (Mario Puzo and Francis Ford Coppola)

OSCAR NOMINATIONS
Best Supporting Actor (James Caan), Best Supporting Actor (Robert Duvall), Best Supporting, Actor (Al Pacino), Best Director (Francis Ford Coppola), Best Editing (William Reynolds, Peter Zinner), Best Costume Design (Anna Hill Johnstone), Best Sound (Bud Grenzbach, Richard Rortman)

THE SCENE
Having taken control of the Corleone family business after the assassination attempt on his father DonVito (Brando), Michael Corleone (Pacino) heads off to Las Vegas with Tom (Duvall) to negotiate the purchase of a casino from shrewd entrepreneur Moe Greene (Alex Rocco), for whom his older brother Fredo (John Cazale) is working. But despite Michael's plan to make Greene "an offer he can't refuse", things don't go terribly well...

unruffled) Is that why you slap my brother around in public?

FREDO: Uh...no, that was nothing, Mike. Now, now Mo didn't mean nothing by that. Sure, he flies off the handle once in a while, but...but Moe and me, we're good friends, right, Moe? Huh?

MOE: *(Ignoring him)* I got a business to run. I gotta kick asses sometimes to make it run right. We had a little argument, Freddie and I, so I had to straighten him out.

MICHAEL: *(Chillingly)* You straightened my brother out?

MOE: He was banging cocktail waitresses two at a time! Players couldn't get a drink at the table! What's wrong with you?

MICHAEL: I leave for New York tomorrow. Think about a price. *(He gets up to leave)*

MOE: Son-of-a-bitch! Do you know who I am? I'm Moe Greene! I made my bones when you were going out with cheerleaders!

FREDO: Wait a minute. Moe, Moe, I got an idea. *(He turns to Tom, who is sitting on the sofa in the corner of the room)* Tom...Tom, you're the consigliere, and you can talk to the Don, you can explain –

TOM: Just a minute now. The Don is semi-retired, and Mike is in charge of the family business now. If you have anything to say, say it to Michael.

(Moe shoots Fredo a threatening look and storms out of the room)

FREDO: *(Furiously)* Mike! You don't come to Las Vegas and talk to a man like Moe Greene like *that!*

MICHAEL: *(Looks up at him levelly)* Fredo. You're my older brother, and I love you. But don't ever take sides with anyone against the family again. Ever...

"Gooood Morning
Vi-et-naaaaaaam!"

Good Morning Vietnam

Goooooooood Mor-ning, Vi-et-naaaaaaam ! Hey, this is not a test, this is rock and *roll*. Time to rock it from the Delta to the DMZ. Is that me or does that sound like an Elvis Presley movie? Oh Viva Da Nang, Dan Nang me, went out to get a rope and hang me...Hey, is it a little too early for being that loud? Hey! Too Late! It's oh six hundred. What's the oh stand for? Oh my God it's early! Speaking of early, how about that Cro-Magnon Marty Dreiwitz? Thank you Marty for "silky smooth sound", make me sound like Peggy Lee...Rock and Roll! Freddie and The Dreamers. Warrrahwahhr... The wronnng speed. Weee've got it onnnn the wronnng speeed. For those of you who are recovering from a hangover that's going to sound just right. Let's put it right back down again. Let's try it a little faster, see if that picks it up a little bit. Let's get it up on 78. nereberegerebrr...those pilots are going Ireallylikethemusic Ireallylikethemusic Ireallylikethemusic. Oh it's still a bad song. Hey, wait a minute. Let's try something. Let's play it backwards and see if it gets any better. Vovchsnyevech. Freddie-is-the-devil Vovchsnyevech. Freddie-is -the-devil.*(Gasps!)* Uh! Na na na na Na na na na Na na na na. Picture a man going on a journey beyond sight and sound. He's left Crete. He's entered...the

Demilitarized Zone Aaaaaah ! De de la, de de la boom. All right! Hey, what is this Demilitarized Zone? What do they mean Police Action? Sounds like a couple of cops in Brooklyn going "Uh, she looks pretty to me". Hey, whatever it is *I like it* because it gets you on your toes better than a strong cup of cappuccino. What is a Demilitarized Zone? Sounds like something out of The Wizard Of Oz. Ohhh nooo! Don't go in there! *(Sings)* Oh He Ho Ho Chi Minh. Ohhh look ! You've landed in Saigon. You're among the little people now. *(Sings)* We represent the RVN Army, the RVN Army. Oh no! Follow the Ho Chi Minh Trail! Follow the Ho Chi Minh Trail! Oh, I'll get you my pretty! Oh my God it's the Wicked Witch of the North! lt's Hanoi Hannah ! Now little G.l. You and your little to-do too ! Ah-hahahahahaha. Oh Adrian. A-dri-an. What're you doing Adrian? Oh, Hannah, you slut! You've been down on everything but the Titanic. Stop it right now...Hey, uh, hi, can you help me? What's your name? My name's Roosevelt Lee Roosevelt. Roosevelt, what town are you stationed in? I'm stationed in Poon Tan. Well thank you, Roosevelt. What's the weather like out there? It's *hot! Damn* hot! *Real* hot! Hot as it is, is my shorts I can cook things in it, a little crotch-pot

cookin'. Well can you tell me what it feels like? *Fool!* Why it's hot I told you again. Were you born on the sun? *It's damn hot!* I said it's so damn hot I saw these little guys in the orange grove burst into flames, it's that hot, you know what I'm talkin' about? What do you think it's going to be like tonight? It's going to be *hot* and *wet*. That's nice if you're with a lady, but it ain't no good if you're in the jungle. Thank you Roosevelt. Here's a song coming your way right now. Nowhere To Run To by Martha And The Vandellas. Yes! Hey, you know what I mean! *(Starts the record.)* *(Off mike to his assistant)* Whew! Too much?

FILM
Good Morning Vietnam (1987)

STARRING
Robin Williams as Adrian Cronauer

WRITER
Mitch Markowitz (additional dialogue ad-libbed by Robin Williams)

DIRECTOR
Barry Levinson

OSCAR NOMINATION
Best Actor

THE SCENE
Vietnam: 1965. D.J. Adrian Cronauer makes his debut broadcast on Armed Forces Radio Saigon...

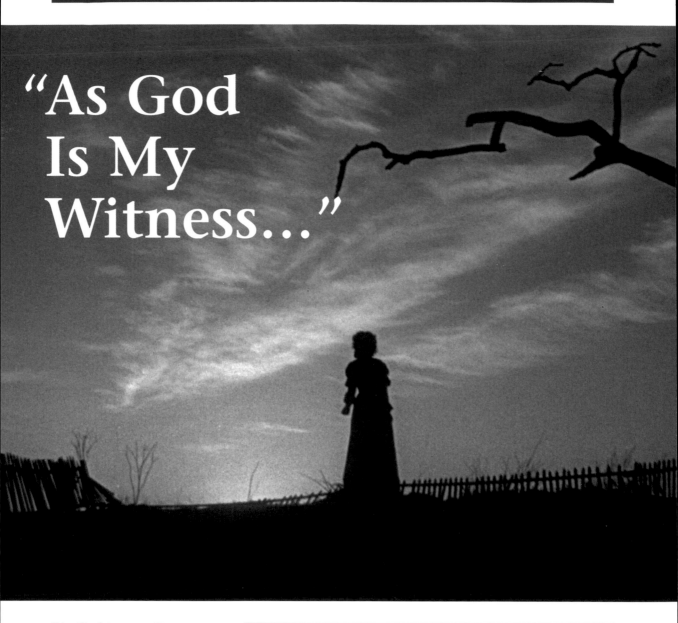

"As God Is My Witness…"

"As God is my witness… as God is my witness, they're not going to lick me! I'm going to live through this, and when it's all over, I'll never be hungry again. No, nor any of my folks! If I have to lie, steal, cheat or kill! As God is my witness, I'll never be hungry again."

FILM
Gone With The Wind (1939)

STARRING
Vivien Leigh as Scarlett O'Hara, Clark Gable as Rhett Butler

WRITER
Sidney Howard, from the novel by Margaret Mitchell

DIRECTOR
Victor Fleming

OSCARS
Best Picture, Best Director, Best Screenplay, Best Actress (Leigh), Best Supporting Actress (Hattie McDaniel), Best Editing, Best Art Direction, Best Cinematography, Award to producer David O.Selznick, Special Award to William Cameron Menzies for outstanding achievement in the use of colour

THE SCENE
Having escaped the burning of Atlanta, Scarlett O'Hara has returned to Tara to find the plantation ravaged by war and her family sick and starving. In the barren fields she makes a vow. This speech is still a popular party piece for every Southern belle in every amateur dramatical society from Virginia to the Gulf of Mexico.

HENRY: You're a pisser. Really funny. You're really funny.

(Pause)

TOMMY: What do you mean I'm funny?

HENRY: It's funny. You know, your, uh...your story; it's funny. You're a funny guy.

(The others fall silent)

TOMMY: You mean the way I talk? What?

HENRY: It's just...you know...you...it's...you're just funny. It's...funny... you know, the way you tell the story and everything.

TOMMY: Funny how? I mean what's funny about it?

ANTHONY: Tommy, no, you got it all wrong.

TOMMY: Whoa, whoa, Anthony. He's a big boy. He knows what he said. What'd you say? Funny how?

HENRY: Ju...just...you know, you're...you're funny.

TOMMY: You mean...let me understand this, 'cause I dunno, maybe it's me, I'm a little fucked up maybe. But I'm funny how? I mean, funny like I'm a clown? I *amuse* you? I make you *laugh*? I'm here to

"Funny How?"

fuckin' amuse you? What do you mean, funny? Funny how? How'm I funny?

HENRY: ...Just, you know, how you tell the story. What?

TOMMY: No. No. I don't know. You said it. How do I know? You said I'm funny. *(Furiously)* How the fuck am I *funny*? What the fuck is so funny about me? Tell me! Tell me what's funny!

(Long pause)

HENRY: Get the fuck outta here Tommy. *(Starts to roar with laughter.)*

TOMMY: You motherfucker. *(They all roar)* I almost had 'im! I almost had 'im! You stutterin' prick, ya! Frankie, was he

shaking? I wonder about you sometimes, Henry. You may fold under questioning!

(Hysterical laughter, Henry wipes tears from his eyes)

FILM
GoodFellas (1990)

WRITERS
Nicholas Pileggi and Martin Scorsese, based on the book Wiseguy by Nicholas Pileggi

DIRECTOR
Martin Scorsese

STARRING
Ray Liotta, Robert DeNiro, Joe Pesci, Lorraine Bracco

OSCAR
Best Supporting Actor (Pesci)

OSCAR NOMINATIONS
Best Picture, Best Direction, Best Supporting Actress (Bracco), Best Adapted Screenplay, Best Editing

THE SCENE
Tommy De Vito (Joe Pesci) is holding court at the Bamboo Lounge with a riotous, foul-mouthed account of a beating he once took from a cop. Fellow wiseguy Henry Hill (Ray Liotta) leads the laughter...

Good Will Hunting

FILM:
Good Will Hunting (1997)

DIRECTOR:
Gus Van Sant

STARRING:
Matt Damon, Robin Williams, Ben Affleck, Minnie Driver

SCREENPLAY:
Matt Damon and Ben Affleck.

THE SCENE:
Will Hunting (Damon), a mathematical genius from the wrong side of the tracks, is offered the chance to study at Harvard on the condition that he see psychologist Sean Maguire (Williams) once a week. Maguire is drubbed by Hunting's massive intellect at their first meeting. The second, however, sees Maguire level the playing field…

(Sean and Will sit on a bench on Boston Common. They look over a small pond, on which a group of schoolchildren on a field trip ride the famous swan boats)

WILL: So what's with this place? You have a swan fetish? Is this something you'd like to talk about?

SEAN: I was thinking about what you said to me the other day, about my painting. I stayed up half the night thinking about it, and then something occurred to me and I fell into a deep, peaceful sleep and haven't thought about you since. You know what occurred to me?

WILL: *(impatient)* No.

SEAN: You're just a boy. You don't have the faintest idea what you're talking about.

WILL: Why, thank you.

SEAN: You've never been out of Boston.

WILL: No.

SEAN: So if I asked you about art you could give me the skinny on every art book ever written…Michaelangelo? You know a lot about him I bet. Life's work, criticisms, political aspirations. But you couldn't tell me what it smells like in the Sistine Chapel. You've never stood there and looked up at that beautiful ceiling. And if I asked you about women I'm sure you could give me a syllabus of your personal favourites, and maybe you've been laid a few times, too. But you couldn't tell me how it feels to wake up next to a woman and be truly happy. If I asked you about war you could refer me to a bevy of fictional and nonfictional material, but you've been in one. You've never held your best friend's head in your lap and watched him draw his last breath, looking to you for help. And if I asked you

"I Don't See A Peer, And I Don't See My Equal. I See A Boy..."

about love I'd get a sonnet, but you've never looked at a woman and been truly vulnerable. Known that someone could kill you with a look. That someone could rescue you from your grief. That God had put an angel on earth just for you. And you wouldn't know how it felt to be her angel. To have the love to be there for her forever. Through anything, through cancer. You wouldn't know about sleeping sitting up in a hospital room for two months holding her hand and not leaving because the doctors could see in your eyes that the term "visiting hours" didn't apply to you. And you wouldn't know about real loss, because that only occurs when you lose something you love more than yourself, and you've never dared to love anything that much. I look at you and I don't see an intelligent, confident man; I don't see a peer, and I don't see my equal. I see a boy...

The Graduate

FILM
The Graduate (1967)

WRITERS
Calder Willingham and Buck Henry, based on the novel by Charles Webb

DIRECTOR
Mike Nichols

STARRING
Dustin Hoffman, Anne Bancroft Katharine Ross

OSCAR
Best Direction

OSCAR NOMINATIONS
Best Picture, Actor (Hoffman), Actress (Bancroft), Supporting Actress (Ross), Writing, Cinematography

THE SCENE
After his welcome home party, Benjamin Braddock (Hoffman) reluctantly ends up alone with Mrs. Robinson (Bancroft), the boozy wife of his father's business partner...

"Mrs. Robinson! You're Trying To Seduce Me!"

BENJAMIN: Look, I think I should be going...

MRS. ROBINSON: Sit down, Benjamin.

BENJAMIN: Mrs. Robinson, if you don't mind my saying so, this conversation is getting a little strange. Now, I'm sure that Mr. Robinson will be here any minute now...

BENJAMIN: Mrs. Robinson, you didn't...I mean, you didn't expect...I mean, you didn't really think I'd do something like that?

BENJAMIN: What do you think?

MRS. ROBINSON: Well, I don't know.

MRS. ROBINSON: No.

BENJAMIN: What?

MRS. ROBINSON: My husband will be back quite late. He should be gone for several hours.

BENJAMIN: Oh my God.

MRS. ROBINSON: Pardon?

BENJAMIN: Oh no, Mrs. Robinson. Oh no!

MRS. ROBINSON: What's wrong?

BENJAMIN: Mrs. Robinson, you didn't...I mean, you didn't expect...I mean you didn't really think I'd do something like *that?*

MRS. ROBINSON: Like what?

BENJAMIN: What do *you* think?

MRS. ROBINSON: Well, I don't know.

BENJAMIN: For God's sake, Mrs. Robinson! Here we are. You got me into your house, you give me a drink, you put on music. Now you start opening up your personal life to me and you tell me your husband won't be home for hours.

MRS. ROBINSON: So?

BENJAMIN: Mrs. Robinson! You're trying to seduce me! *(She laughs)*

BENJAMIN: *(Unsure)...Aren't you?*

"I'll Be There!"

"Well, maybe it's like Casey says. A fella ain't got a soul of his own, just a little piece of a big soul, the one big soul that belongs to ever'body. I'll be all around in the dark. I'll be ever'where, wherever you can look. Wherever there's a fight so hungry people can eat, I'll be there. Wherever there's a cop beatin' up a guy, I'll be there. I'll be in the way guys yell when they're mad, and I'll be in the way kids laugh when they're hungry an' they know supper's ready. An' when the people are eatin' the stuff they raise, livin' in the houses they build, I'll be there too."

FILM
The Grapes Of Wrath (1940)

DIRECTOR
John Ford

SCREENPLAY
Nunnally Johnson (adapted from the novel by John Steinbeck)

STARRING
Henry Fonda, Jane Darwell, John Carradine

OSCARS
Best Direction (Ford), Best Supporting Actress (Darwell)

OSCAR NOMINATIONS
Best Picture, Actor (Fonda), Screenplay, Editing, Sound Recording

THE SCENE
The fugitive Tom Joad says his final farewell to his heartbroken Ma...

"And That's How I Found Out There Was No Santa Claus..."

KATE: Now I have another reason to hate Christmas.

BILLY: What are you talking about?

KATE: The worst thing that ever happened to me was on Christmas. God, it was so horrible. It was Christmas Eve. I was nine years old. Me and mom were decorating the tree, waiting for dad to come home from work. Couple of hours went by, dad wasn't home, so mom called the office. No answer. Christmas Day came and went, and still nothing. The police began a search. Four or five days went by. Neither one of us could eat or sleep. Everything was falling apart. It was snowing outside. The house was freezing, so I went to try to light up the fire. And that's when I noticed the smell. Firemen came, broke through the chimney top. Then me and mom were expecting them to pull out a dead cat or a bird, and instead they pulled out my father. He was dressed in a Santa Claus suit. He'd been climbing down the chimney on Christmas Eve. His arm was loaded with presents. He was gonna surprise us. He slipped and broke his neck, died instantly. And that's how I found out there was no Santa Claus...

FILM
Gremlins (1984)

DIRECTOR
Joe Dante

STARRING
Zach Galligan, Phoebe Cates, Hoyt Axton

SCREENPLAY
Chris Columbus

THE SCENE
Under siege by the Gremlins in the sleepy town of Kingston on Christmas Eve, Billy (Zach Galligan) and Gizmo the Mogwai are agog as Kate (Phoebe Cates) relates her tragic tale...

"I Fought The War For Your Sort..."

(A fifth passenger, a middle class gentleman enters the train compartment. The Beatles nod their hellos but the gentleman ignores them and begins reading his newspaper. Shortly, he stands and shuts the window)

PAUL: Do you mind if we have it open?

PASSENGER: Yes, I do.

JOHN: Yeah, but there's four of us and we'd like it open – if it's all the same to you, that is.

(He bats his eyelashes)

PASSENGER: It isn't. I travel on this train regularly. Twice a week. So I suppose I have some rights.

RINGO: So have we!

(The gentleman ignores him and resumes reading his newspaper. Opposite him, Ringo decides to put his radio on. At full blast)

PASSENGER: *(Leaning forward to switch the radio off again)* And we'll have that thing off as well, thank you.

RINGO: But –

PASSENGER: I have an elementary knowledge of the railway. I should tell you that I'm perfectly within my rights.

PAUL: Yeah, but we wanna hear it. There's more of us than you. We're a community. Charity vote! Up the workers and all that stuff.

PASSENGER: Then I suggest you take that damn thing into the corridor or some other part of the train where you obviously belong.

JOHN: *(Leaning close)* Give us a kiss…

PAUL: Look, mister, we paid for our seats too, you know.

PASSENGER: I travel on this train regularly. Twice a week.

JOHN: Knock it off, Paul. You can't win with his sort. After all, it's his train – isn't it mister?

PASSENGER: And don't take that tone with me young man. I fought the war for your sort.

RINGO: I bet you're sorry you won…

FILM
A Hard Day's Night (1964)

DIRECTOR
Richard Lester

STARRING
John Lennon, Paul McCartney, George Harrison, Ringo Starr

SCREENPLAY
Alun Owen

OSCAR NOMINATIONS
Best Screenplay, Best Score

THE SCENE
After escaping a stampede of slavering pubescent school girls, the Fab Four board a train at Liverpool Lime Street station only to face the wrath of a middle-aged gentleman passenger (Richard Vernon) who is decidedly unimpressed with the mopheads' cheeky charm…

(Hanna and McCauley face each other across a table. They don't appear to drink coffee. They don't eat. They look each other in the eye sporadically but their eyes frequently dart around the coffee shop as they talk and listen)

HANNA: Seven years in Folsom. In the hole for three. McNeil before that. McNeil as tough as they say?

McCAULEY: You looking to become a panologist?

HANNA: You lookin' to go back. You know, I chase down some crews, guys just looking to fuck up, get busted back…that you?

McCAULEY: You must've worked some dipshit crews.

HANNA: I've worked all kinds.

McCAULEY:… You see me doing thrill seeker liquor store hold-ups with a Born To Lose tattoo on my chest?

HANNA: No, I do not.

McCAULEY: Right *(pause)* I ain't never *going* back.

HANNA: Then don't take down scores.

McCAULEY: I do what I do best. I take down scores. You'll do what you do best: try to stop guys like me.

HANNA: So you never wanted a regular-type life?

McCAULEY: The fuck is that? Barbecues and Ballgames?

HANNA: *(pause)* Yeah.

McCAULEY: This regular-type life – that your life?

HANNA: My life? No…My life's a disaster zone, I got a stepdaughter so fucked-up because her real father's this large-type asshole. I got a wife. We're passing each other on the down slope of a marriage – my third – because I spend all my time chasing guys like you around the block. That's my life.

McCAULEY: Guy told me one time, don't let yourself get attached to anything you are not willing to walk out on in 30 seconds flat if you feel the heat around the corner. Now, if you're around me and you've gotta move when I move, how do you expect to keep a…a marriage?

HANNA: That's an interesting point. What are you, a monk?

McCAULEY: I have a woman.

HANNA: What do you tell her?

McCAULEY: I tell her I'm a salesman.

HANNA: *(long pause)* So then, if you spot me comin' round the corner, you just gonna walk out on this woman? Not say goodbye?

McCAULEY: That's the discipline.

HANNA: That's pretty vacant.

McCAULEY: It's what it is. It's that or we both better go do something else, pal.

HANNA: I don't know how to do anything else.

McCAULEY: Neither do I.

(A look passes between them. They both struggle to keep from smiling)

HANNA: You know, I have this recurring dream. I'm sitting at this big banquet table and all the victims of all the murders I ever worked are sitting at this

---

FILM
Heat (1995)

DIRECTOR
Michael Mann

STARRING
Al Pacino, Robert DeNiro, Val Kilmer, Tom Sizemore

SCREENPLAY
Michael Mann

THE SCENE
LAPD tough guy detective Vincent Hanna (Pacino) has been closing in on hesitmeister Neil McCauley (DeNiro). Hanna sets up McCauley for a major fall by staking out his gang's next target – but McCauley, sensing the "heat", coolly walks away into the night. Frustrated, Hanna tails McCauley on the freeway, flags him down and suggests he buy him a coffee…

"That's My Life…"

table and they're staring at me with these black eyeballs, 'cause they got eight-ball haemorrhages. In the head wounds. And there they are, these big balloon people, I found them two weeks after they'd been under the bed. The neighbours reported the smell. And there they are. All of them just sitting there.

McCAULEY: What do they say?

HANNA: Nothin'.

McCAULEY: No talk.

HANNA: No just…They don't have anything to say. They just look at each other. They look at me and that's it, that's the dream. *(Snaps his fingers)*

McCAULEY: I have one where I'm drowning and I've got to wake myself up and start breathing or I'll die in my sleep.

HANNA: You know what that's about?

McCAULEY: Yeah, having enough time.

HANNA: Enough time…to do what you wanna do?

McCAULEY: That's right.

HANNA: You doin' it now?

McCAULEY: Not there yet.

HANNA: You know, we're sitting here, you and I, like a couple of regular fellas. You do what you do. I do what I gotta do. And now that we've been face to

face, if I'm there and I gotta put you away, I won't like it. But I'll tell ya, if it's between you and some poor bastard whose wife you're gonna turn into a widow, brother, you are going down.

McCAULEY: *(long pause)* There's a flip side to that coin. What if you do got me boxed in, and I gotta put you down? 'Cause no matter what, you will not get in my way. We've been face to face, yeah, but I will not hesitate, not for a second.

HANNA: Maybe that's the way it'll be. Or…who knows?

McCAULEY: Or, maybe, we'll never see each other again…

"I Got Oil In My Arm"

FILM
The Hustler (1961)

DIRECTOR
Robert Rossen

SCREENPLAY
Sidney Carroll and Robert Rossen
(adapted from the novel by Walter Tevis)

STARRING
Paul Newman, Piper Laurie, Jackie Gleason

OSCARS
Cinematography (Eugen Shuftan), Art Direction/Set
Decoration (Harry Horner, Gene Callahan)

OSCAR NOMINATIONS
Best Picture, Actor (Newman), Actress (Laurie),
Supporting Actor (Gleason)

THE SCENE
Fast Eddie Felson explains the buzz he gets out of
playing pool...

"Anything can be great. I don't care, bricklaying can be great if a guy knows, if he knows what he's doing and why, and if he can make it come off. When I'm goin', I mean when I'm really goin', I feel like a, like a jockey must feel sitting on his horse. He's got all that speed and that power underneath him, he's comin' into the stretch, the pressure's on him. And he knows, just feels, when to let it go, how much. 'Cause he's got everything working for him, timing, touch. It's a great feeling, boy, a real great feeling, when you're right and you know you're right. Like all of a sudden I got oil in my arm. Pool cue's part of me. You know, it's a...pool cue has got nerves in it. It's a piece of wood, it's got nerves in it. You can feel the roll of those balls. You don't have to look. You just know. You make shots that nobody's ever made before. And you play that game the way nobody's ever played it before."

In Which We Serve

"If They Had To Die, What A Grand Way To Go!"

CAPTAIN KINROSS: Come a little closer *(The men shuffle towards him)*...I have to say goodbye to the few of you who are left. We had so many talks, and this is our last. I've always tried to crack a joke or two before, and you've all been friendly and laughed at them. But today, I'm afraid I've run out of jokes; and I don't suppose any of us feels much like laughing.

The Torrin has been in one scrap after another, but even when we've had men killed, the majority survived and brought the old ship back. Now, she lies in 1,500 fathoms. And with her, more than half our shipmates. If they had to die, what a grand way to go! For now they lie all together with the ship we loved and

they're in very good company. We've lost her, but they're still with her.

There may be less than half the Torrin left. But I feel that we all take up the battle with even stronger heart; each of us knows twice as much about fighting, and each of us has twice as much reason to fight.

You will all be sent to replace men who've been killed in other ships And the next time you're in action, remember the Torrin. *(He's on the verge of blubbing)* I should like to add that there isn't one of you that I wouldn't be proud and honoured to serve with again. Goodbye and good luck. And thank you all from the bottom of my heart...

FILM
In Which We Serve (1942)

DIRECTORS
Noel Coward and David Lean

STARRING
Noel Coward, John Mills, Bernard Miles, Celia Johnson, Kay Walsh, Joyce Carey, Michael Wilding, Richard Attenborough

SCREENPLAY
Noel Coward

OSCARS
Outstanding Production Achievement for Noel Coward

OSCAR NOMINATIONS
Best Picture, Best Original Screenplay

THE SCENE
As his ship, the HMS Torrin, lies at the bottom of the ocean, Captain E. V. Kinross (Noel Coward) emotionally addresses his broken and severely depleted crew for the last time, displaying his ever-caring, ever-fatherly nature. The dialogue was based on an actual speech given by Lord Mountbatten to his own crew on HMS Kelly. The film won its co-star, co-director, writer, musical scorer, and general one-man-band Noel Coward a special achievement Oscar from the Academy for "outstanding production..."

"I'm A Free Man And I'm Going Out The Front Door..."

JUDGE: Silence! *(Bangs gavel furiously)* In the matter of Her Majesty versus Gerard Partick Conlon, the case is hereby dismissed.

(The courtroom erupts with cheering and applause, carnations are thrown into the air. Conlon embraces Pierce while amid the furore, his mother (Maureen McBride) shouts unheard at the judge)

MOTHER: My husband died in your prison an innocent man!

CONLON: *(Quietly, to those around him)* I'll see you outside...I'll see you outside.

(Conlon ignores the policeman who is trying to usher him out another way, and climbs onto the tiers of benches rising behind him. Everyone looks up at him and the crowd cheers as he walks to the back of the court)

PIERCE: *(To the judge)* What about Guiseppe Conlon? Your Honour, he was an innocent man.

(Conlon, meanwhile, has reached the door of the courtroom where the police try again to persuade him to use the building's rear exit)

CONLON: I'm a free man and I'm going out the front door.

JUDGE: In the matter of Her Majesty versus Paul Hill, the case is hereby dismissed.

(There is renewed cheering. Cuts between Conlon striding toward the front door – surrounded by photographers with flash guns, triumphantly throwing his jacket to the floor – and the courtroom)

HILL: *(Shrugging off the police)* Leave me alone, I'm going out the front with Gerry.

JUDGE: In the matter of Her Majesty versus Partick Armstrong, the case is hereby dismissed.

(Armstrong stands and silently accepts the crowd's applause)

FILM
In The Name Of The Father (1993)

DIRECTOR
Jim Sheridan

STARRING
Daniel Day-Lewis, Pete Postlethwaite, Emma Thompson

SCREENPLAY
Terry George, Jim Sheridan

OSCAR NOMINATIONS
Best Picture, Best Director, Best Screenplay, Best Actor (Daniel Day-Lewis), Best Supporting Actor (Pete Postlethwaite), Best Supporting Actress (Emma Thompson), Best Editing

THE SCENE
After the IRA kill five people in the 1974 Guildford pub bombings, Gerard Conlon (Day-Lewis), Paul Hill (John Lynch), Patrick 'Paddy' Armstrong (Mark Sheppard) and Carole Richardson (Beatie Edney) are wrongly accused of and imprisoned for murder. Conlon's father Guiseppe is among seven other innocents also falsely imprisoned as part of their supposed "support unit". When a real IRA man is jailed in the same wing as the Conlons, he tells Gerry that he has told the British authorities that he committed the crime for which they are serving time. Solicitor Gareth Pierce (Thompson) campaigns with Conlon and his father to see that justice is done but, tragically, Guiseppe dies before Pierce can discover the evidence – withheld at the original trial – that will prove the verdict was a sham. Pierce presents the new evidence to the Court Of Appeal and, after retiring to consider his verdict, the judge (Denys Hawthorne) returns to his courtroom amid chaotic and noisy scenes...

JUDGE: In the matter of Her Majesty versus Carole Richardson, the case is hereby dismissed.

(Conlon is outside now, surrounded by cameras, microphones and well-wishers, and takes the opportunity to make his impassioned promise)

CONLON: *(Tremulously, his voice clear but close to cracking with emotion)* I'm an innocent man. I spent 15 years in prison for something I didn't do. I watched my father die in a British prison for something he didn't do. And this government still says he's guilty. I want to tell them that until my father is proved innocent, until all the people involved in this case are proved innocent, until the guilty ones are brought to justice, I will fight on in the name of my father and of the truth…

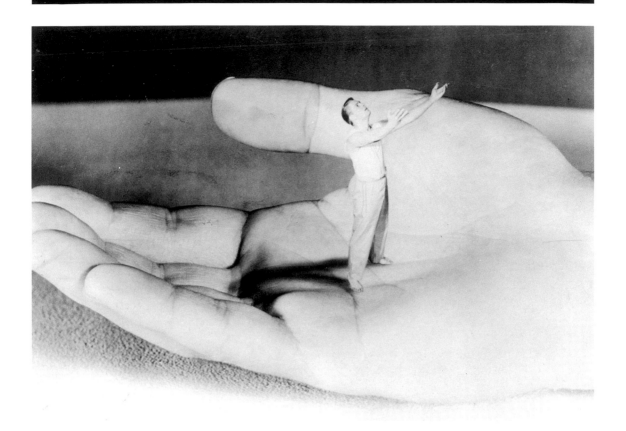

"I Meant Something Too!"

I was continuing to shrink, to become…what? The infinitesimal? What was I? Still a human being, or was I the man of the future? If there were other bursts of radiation, other clouds drifting across cities and continents, would other beings follow me into this vast new world? So close, the infinitesimal and the infinite. But suddenly I knew they were really the two ends of the same concept. The unbelievably small and the unbelievably vast eventually meet, like the closing of a gigantic circle. I looked up, as if somehow I would grasp the heavens, the universe, worlds beyond number, God's silver tapestry spread across the night. And in that moment I knew the answer to the riddle of the infinite. I had thought in terms of man's own limited dimension. I had presumed upon nature. That existence begins and ends is *man's* conception, not nature's. And I felt my body dwindling, melting, becoming nothing. My fears melted away, and in their place came acceptance. All this vast majesty of creation, it had to mean something. And then I meant something too. Yes, smaller than the smallest, I meant something too! To God, there is no zero. I still exist!

FILM
The Incredible Shrinking Man (1957)

STARRING
Grant Williams as Robert Scott Carey

SCREENPLAY
Richard Matheson (from his novel)

DIRECTOR
Jack Arnold

THE SCENE
Exposure to radiation and insecticide has altered Robert Scott Carey's molecular structure, and he gradually shrinks to the size of an insect…

"I Want To Live Again..."

FILM
It's A Wonderful Life (1946)

WRITERS
Frances Goodrich, Albert Hackett and Frank Capra

DIRECTOR
Frank Capra

STARRING
James Stewart, Donna Reed, Lionel Barrymore, Henry Travers

OSCAR NOMINATIONS
Best Picture, Best Direction, Best Actor, Sound Recording, Film Editing

THE SCENE
The "never born" George Bailey runs on to the bridge pleading for heavenly help after seeing what his world would have become without him...

Clarence! Clarence! *(He clasps his hands in prayer)* Help me, Clarence! Get me back! Get me back, I don't care what happens to me. Get me back to my wife and kids. Help me, Clarence, please. Please. I want to live again. *(He cries)* I want to live again. Please God, let me live again. *(Bert the policeman arrives and George realises his prayer has been answered)* Merry Christmas! Mary! Mary! Yay! Yay! Hello Bedford Falls! *(He runs, hysterical and exuberant, through the middle of the town)* Merry Christmas! Merry Christmas, movie house! Merry Christmas, emporium! Merry Christmas, you wonderful old Building and Loan! Hey! Merry Christmas, Mr Potter!

"Hang On A Minute, Lads. I've Got A Great Idea..."

CHARLIE: Hold still, hold still, hold still, hold still!

(Everyone freezes on the spot at his command)

CHARLIE: Nobody move.

(They stay still)

CHARLIE: We're balancing right on the edge. Very slowly move this way. Very slowly. Don't make a sharp movement...Come as far this way as you can get.

(The bewildered robbers start edging gingerly toward the "safer" front end of the coach, replacing silly hats, putting on shoes and claiming beer bottles as they go. The coach lurches dangerously)

CHARLIE: Watch it! Watch it...Watch it, Bill!

(The bus tilts some more and the pile of gold slides frustratingly away from them)

CHARLIE: The gold is

pulling it over the edge. We'll have to get it back.

(Charlie creeps slowly toward the stolen gold. His dim-witted cohorts follow. The coach tips precariously)

CHARLIE: Get back! Get back!

FILM
The Italian Job (1969)

DIRECTOR
John Collinson

STARRING
Michael Caine, Noel Coward, Benny Hill, Raf Vallone, Tony Beckley, Rossano Brazi, Maggie Blye

SCREENPLAY
Tony Kennedy Martin

THE SCENE
Charlie Coker (Caine) and his gang have successfully pulled off the crime caper of the century – organised by incarcerated but dapper English villain Mr. Bridger (Coward) – nabbing $4,000,000 worth of Italian gold bullion from under the noses not only of the police, but of the Mafia as well; right

in the middle of a Milan congested with post-international football traffic, to boot. Disposing of their swish red, white and blue Mini Coopers on the way, they are now jubilantly heading for freedom through the Italian Alps in a gutted coach, and the party atmosphere reaches irresponsible heights. With the pile of gold at one end and the boisterous revellers at the other, the coach begins to take the dicey mountain corners at increasingly greater speed. Then, somewhat inevitably, disaster strikes. The customised coach swerves out of control, crashes through the barrier by the side of the road, and comes to a halt dangling half on, half off, the mountain road. The drop is a very long way indeed. There is a stunned silence. The vehicle gently seesaws up and down...

(They shuffle back in panic)

CHARLIE: Now hold still, don't move, don't move at all. Don't no one get out of the bus, *neevah*! Otherwise we'll all go.

(Charlie manages to lower himself to all fours and begins to crawl forward, but the coach continues its seesawing and the bullion slides away from him)

CHARLIE: (Gesturing) Edge back as far as you can go. To coun – (The coach takes a frightening lurch)…to counterbalance me now.

(The coach tips back safely again. Charlie slowly crawls forward again, almost reaching the gold but it slips away again, out of reach. There is a pause. Then Charlie turns to his cronies)

CHARLIE: Hang on a minute, lads. I've got a great idea…er…er…

"I Have Trouble With My Sinuses..."

KAA:
(Sitting in the tree with Mowgli when Shere Khan yanks on his tail) Oh, now what? I'll be right down! *(He slithers down from the tree and looks around, but there is no one there)* Yes, yes? Who is it?

SHERE KHAN: *(Appears from behind the tree)* It's me, Shere Khan. I'd like a word with you, if you don't mind.

KAA: Shere Khan! What a surprise!

SHERE KHAN: Yes, isn't it? I just dropped by. Forgive me if I've interrupted anything.

KAA: Oh no, no, nothing at all.

SHERE KHAN: I thought perhaps you were entertaining someone up there in your coils *(Snaps open his claws and begins drumming on the ground impatiently)*

KAA: *(Panicky)* Coils? Someone? Oh no – I was just curling up for my siesta.

SHERE KHAN: But you were singing to someone. Who is it, Kaa?

(He reaches out and grabs him by the throat)

KAA: Who? No, no. I was just singing, er, to myself.

SHERE KHAN: Indeed.

KAA: Yes. Yes. You see, I *(Gulps for breath)* have trouble with my sinuses.

SHERE KHAN: *(In mock sympathy)* What a pity.

(He releases his grip on Kaa's neck)

KAA: Oh, you have no idea. It's simply terrible. I can't eat, I can't sleep, so I sing myself to sleep. You know, self-hypnosis? *(He slithers up towards Shere Khan, eyes blazing hypnotically)* Let me show you how it works. *(Starts to sing)* Tru-st in me...

(Bored, Shere Khan swats Kaa's head to the ground)

SHERE KHAN: Oh no, I can't be bothered with that. I've no time for that nonsense.

KAA: *(Gasping for breath)* Some other time, perhaps?

SHERE KHAN: Perhaps. But at the moment I'm searching for a man cub.

KAA: *(Sits up in alarm)* Man cub? What man cub?

SHERE KHAN: The one who's lost. Now, where do you suppose he could be?

KAA: Search me.

(Recoils in alarm as he realises what he's said)

SHERE KHAN: That's an excellent idea. I'm sure you wouldn't mind showing me your coils, would you Kaa?

KAA: Er, certainly not. *(He lowers his tail from the tree)* Nothing here. And nothing *(He opens his mouth and points out its apparent emptiness with his tail)* in here.

(Up in the tree, Mowgli snores)

KAA: *(Imitating the snore)* My sinuses!

SHERE KHAN: Hmmmm. Indeed. And now, how about the middle?

KAA: The middle? Oh, the middle! *(He partially uncoils himself from around Mowgli and lowers the middle part of his body down. Shere Khan prods it suspiciously)* Absolutely nothing in the middle!

SHERE KHAN: Hmmmmm. Really? Well, if you do just happen to see the man cub, you will inform me first. Understand?

(He scratches Kaa threateningly under the chin with a single claw)

KAA: *(Gulps)* I get the point *(He coils himself up into a knot)* Cross my heart. Hope to die.

SHERE KHAN: Good show. And now I must continue my search for the helpless little lad...

FILM
The Jungle Book (1967)

DIRECTOR
Wolfgang Reitherman

VOICES
Phil Harris (Baloo The Bear), Bruce Reitherman (Mowgli), George Sanders (Shere Khan), Sterling Holloway (Kaa), Sebastian Cabot (Bagheera), Louis Prima (King Louie)

SCREENPLAY
Larry Clemmons, Ralph Wright, Ken Anderson, Vance Gerry

OSCAR NOMINATIONS
Terry Gilkison (Best Song)

THE SCENE
Fearing that Mowgli the man cub (Reitherman) is in danger after the man-hating tiger Shere Khan (Sanders) returns to the jungle, the boy's animal friends Bagheera (Cabot) and Baloo (Harris) attempt to return him to the safety of the man village. En route Mowgli runs away, is entrapped by the crafty snake Kaa (Holloway) and hypnotised into a slumber. Unfortunately for Kaa, while the lad snoozes peacefully wrapped in the snake's coils up a tree, Shere Khan cottons on to the fact that the serpent may have company of the human variety and decides to pay him a visit...

"The Thing About A Shark..."

"Japanese submarine slammed two torpedoes into our side, chief...just delivered the Bomb, the Hiroshima Bomb. Eleven hundred men went into the water. The vessel went down in 12 minutes. Didn't see the first shark for about half an hour. Tiger. Thirteen footer. You know how you know that when you're in the water, chief? You can tell by looking from the dorsal to the tail. What we didn't know was our bomb mission had been so secret, no distress signal had been sent. They didn't even list us overdue for a week. Very first light, chief, sharks come cruisin'. So we formed ourselves into tight groups, you know kinda like old squares in a battle like you see in a calendar, like the Battle Of Waterloo, and the idea was the shark comes to the nearest man and you pound and holler and scream and sometimes the shark'd go away. Sometimes he *wouldn't* go away. Sometimes that shark, he looks right into you...right into your eyes. You know the thing about a shark, he's got lifeless eyes, black eyes, like a *doll's* eyes. When he comes at you he doesn't seem to be living...until he bites...and those black eyes roll over white and then...aw, then you hear that terrible high pitched screamin', the ocean turns red, and in spite of all the poundin' and hollerin' they all come in and they...rip you to pieces..."

FILM
Jaws (1975)

DIRECTOR
Steven Spielberg

WRITERS
Peter Benchley, Carl Gottlieb, John Milius (based upon the novel by Peter Benchley)

STARRING
Roy Scheider, Robert Shaw, Richard Dreyfuss

OSCARS
Best Score (John Williams), Best Editing (Verna Fields), Best Sound

OSCAR NOMINATIONS
Best Picture

THE SCENE
Grizzly old shark hunter Quint (Shaw) explains his obsession to police chief Brody (Scheider) and marine biologist Hooper (Dreyfuss) by recounting the real-life horror of the sinking of the U.S.S Indianapolis...

"It's Supposed To Be About Justice"

(Vincennes' office. Jack is looking at the latest cover of gossip magazine Hush-Hush when Exley bursts through the door)

EXLEY: Vincennes, I need your help on something.

VINCENNES: I'm busy right now. Why don't you just go and ask some of your boys on homicide.

EXLEY: I can't. I need someone outside of homicide. I want you to tail Bud White 'til he goes on duty this evening.

VINCENNES: Why don't you do me a real favour and leave me alone.

EXLEY: Do you make the three negroes for the Night Owl killings?

VINCENNES: *(pause)* What?

EXLEY: It's a simple question.

VINCENNES: Why in the world do you want to go digging any deeper into the Night Owl Killings, Lieutenant?

EXLEY: Rollo Timassi.

VINCENNES: Is there more to that or am I supposed to guess?

EXLEY: Rollo was a purse-snatcher. *(pause)* My father ran into him off duty...and he shot my father six times and got away clean. No one even knew who he was...I just made the name up to give him some personality.

VINCENNES: What's your point?

EXLEY: Rollo Timassi is the reason I became a cop. I wanted to catch the guys who thought they could get away with it. It's supposed to be about justice. Then somehow, along the way, I lost sight of that...Why did you become a cop?

VINCENNES: *(long pause)* I don't remember. What do you want, Exley?

EXLEY: I just wanna solve this thing.

VINCENNES: Night Owl was solved.

EXLEY: No, I wanna do it right.

VINCENNES: Even if it means paying the consequences?

EXLEY: Uh-huh.

VINCENNES: Alright, college boy, I'll help. But there's a case your boys on homicide don't care about. They think it's just another Hollywood *homo*-cide. But I don't. You help me with mine, I'll help you with yours. Deal?

EXLEY: Deal.

FILM
LA Confidential (1997)

DIRECTOR
Curtis Hanson

STARRING
Kevin Spacey, Guy Pierce, Russell Crowe, Kim Basinger

SCREENPLAY
Brian Helgeland and Curtis Hanson

THE SCENE
Clean-cut Detective Ed Exley (Pierce) finds himself embroiled in a mystery case that links the renowned escort agency Fleur De Lis and the shocking Night Owl killings with the inner circle of the LAPD. In desperation, he seeks help from a celebrity crime-stopper Jack Vincennes (Spacey) a corrupt cop wrestling with a conscience...

"You Don't Eat Things With Names..."

(Mac and Oldsen are tucking into dinner. Soft classical music plays in the background. Gordon comes out of the kitchen and pours the pair some more wine)

OLDSEN: (To Gordon) Excuse me, could I have another roll please?

GORDON: Certainly.

MAC: (To Gordon) We saw an old man on the beach today. Who was that?

GORDON: Oh, that'd be Ben.

MAC: Is that his shack?

GORDON: Yes.

MAC: And he lives there the whole year?

GORDON: Oh yes.

MAC: Doesn't he get cold?

GORDON: No, he's used to it. How's the Casserole de Lapin ?

MAC: Excellent, terrific, thank you.

(Gordon goes back into the kitchen. Mac continues eating, but Oldsen has been visibly disturbed by this last question)

OLDSEN: Lapin. That's rabbit.

(Mac stops eating mid-mouthful and looks at Oldsen, alarmed. Gordon returns from the *kitchen with the bread basket)*

MAC: *(To Gordon)* Is this my rabbit?

GORDON: *(Unperturbed)* Yes.

(Mac spits out his mouthful in disgust)

OLDSEN: *(Mournfully)* Harry.

MAC: Trudy.

GORDON: *(Calmly)* We don't allow animals in the bedrooms. I should have told you sooner.

(Stella emerges from the kitchen)

MAC: It was a pet, not an animal. It had a name – you don't eat things with names! This is horrific!

GORDON: *(Still unruffled)* It was an injured rabbit, that's all. It was in shock with a broken leg. It was in pain.

OLDSEN: *(To Gordon)* Excuse me, Mr. Urquhart, but I think you're a bit hasty. Mac was looking after it. All it needed was lots of rest and the proper treatment. There was every chance of a full recovery and a fully active life. Mac was on top of the situation.

GORDON: *(To Stella)* They didn't like the rabbit.

OLDSEN: Mac loved the rabbit, that's just the point. *(Getting up)* It had a name! Two names! *(He stalks out of the room)*

GORDON: I'm sorry. I don't think there's a lot I can do, though. Is it worthwhile calling the vet still?

STELLA: Don't be a clown, Gordon. Get into the kitchen and make some coffee.

GORDON: It had a broken leg. It was a clean snap. You check the bones in the

dish if you don't believe me.

(He goes back into the kitchen. Stella sits down beside Mac, who is examining the broken bones in the casserole dish)

STELLA: *(Sympathetically)* I'm sorry, Mac, but we eat rabbits here. The vet would have done the same. I didn't know it had a name.

MAC: It's okay, Stella.

STELLA: Oh look, you don't have to finish it if you don't want to. How was it anyway?

MAC: It was nice. Apart from it being Trudy, It was nice.

STELLA: What lovely long eyelashes you've got. *(Mac sits back in surprise. There is an uneasy silence)*

MAC: Was it in a wine sauce?

STELLA: Yeah. Yeah, I just let it simmer for a couple of hours in some white wine. Why did you call it Trudy?

MAC: No reason…

FILM
Local Hero (1983)

DIRECTOR
Bill Forsyth

STARRING
Peter Riegert, Burt Lancaster, Peter Capaldi, Denis Lawson, Fulton Mackay, Jenny Seagrove, Jennifer Black

SCREENPLAY
Bill Forsyth

THE SCENE
Mac (Riegert), working for a Texan oil firm, has been shipped off to a remote Scottish town, not only to buy the place for North Sea oil drilling but also to watch the skies for his astronomy-fixated boss Happer (Lancaster). En route to the town, he and his Scottish colleague Oldsen (Capaldi) rescue an injured rabbit from the roadside, which Mac shelters in his hotel room. However, in their efforts to buy up the town, a task which proves easier than they first suspected, the animal is forgotten – until the pair are having dinner in their hotel one night served by Gordon (Lawson) and his wife Stella (Black) …

The Long Good Friday

"Touch Of The Dunkirk Spirit, Know What I Mean?"

(There is a brief argument during which the two Americans compare Shand's "troubles" to the St. Valentine's Day Massacre and a bad day in Vietnam)

SHAND: *(Deflated)* Bon voyage then. *(He stops at the door, then turns back)* I'll tell you something. *(Now cocksure and happier)* I'm glad I found out in time just what a partnership with a pair of wankers like you would've been like. A sleeping partner's one thing but you're in a fucking *coma*! No wonder you got an energy crisis your side of the water. Us British, we're used to a bit more vitality, imagination, touch of the Dunkirk spirit, know what I mean? The days when Yanks could come over here and buy up Nelson's Column and a Harley Street surgeon and a coupla Windmill girls are definitely over...

AMERICAN #2: Now look...

SHAND: *(Hisses)* Shut up you long streak of paralysed piss. What I'm looking for is someone who can *contribute* to what England has given to the world. Culture, sophistication, genius...a little bit more than an 'ot dog, know what I mean? We're in the Common Market now, and my new deal is with Europe. I'm going into partnership with a German organisation.

Yeah, the *Krauts*! They've got ambition, know-how. And they don't lose their bottle. The Mafia? Hahahaha. I shit 'em...

FILM
The Long Good Friday (1980)

DIRECTOR
John Mackenzie

STARRING
Bob Hoskins, Helen Mirren, Dave King, Derek Thompson

THE SCENE
London gang boss Harold Shand's (Hoskins) attempts to woo the American Mafia to invest in his multi-million pound building project have, over the course of the titular public holiday, gone horribly awry. Two bombs have destroyed his pub and Rolls Royce, a third has been discovered in his casino, and a number of his gang have been slaughtered. After learning that his own consort (Thompson) had betrayed him to the IRA, Shand brutally murders him then hurries back to the Savoy hotel where his American "friends", appalled by the violence, are preparing to leave...

FILM
Manhattan (1979)

DIRECTOR
Woody Allen

STARRING
Woody Allen, Diane Keaton, Michael Murphy, Mariel Hemingway, Meryl Streep, Anne Byrne, Karen Ludwig, Michael O'Donoghue, Victor Truro, Tina Farrow

SCREENPLAY
Woody Allen and Marshall Brickman

OSCAR NOMINATIONS
Supporting Actress (Hemingway), Original Screenplay

THE SCENE
In Manhattan's memorable opening monologue, as scenes of New York pass before our eyes and Gershwin massages our ear-drums, well-known scribe Isaac Davis speaks into a dictaphone, planning the first chapter of his new book…

"New York Was His Town And It Always Would be…"

ISAAC: "Chapter One: He adored New York City. He idolised it all out of proportion." Uh, no, make that, "He, he *romanticised* it all out of proportion." Better. "To him, no matter what the season was, this was still a town that existed in black and white and pulsated to the great tunes of George Gershwin." Er, no, let me start this over…

"Chapter One: He was too romantic about Manhattan, as he was about everything else. He thrived on the hustle-bustle of the crowds and the traffic. To him, New York meant beautiful women and street-smart guys who seemed to know all the angles." Nah, no…corny, too corny for, you know, my taste. Let me, let me try to be more profound…

"Chapter One: He adored New York City. To him it was a metaphor for the decay of contemporary culture. The same lack of individual integrity that caused so many people to take the easy way out was rapidly turning the town of his dreams…" It's gonna be too preachy, I mean, you know, let's face it, I wanna sell some books here…

"Chapter One: He adored New York City. Although to him it was a metaphor for the decay of contemporary culture. How hard it was to exist in a society desensitised by drugs, loud music, television, crime, garbage…" Too angry. I don't wanna be angry…

"Chapter One: He was as tough and romantic as the city he loved. Behind his black-rimmed glasses was the coiled sexual power of a jungle cat." I love this. "New York was his town. And it always would be…"

Marathon Man

"A Live, Freshly Cut Nerve Is Infinitely More Sensitive..."

SZELL: *(Szell begins his methodical preparations by lifting a briefcase onto the table in front of Babe and opening it)* You know the value of diamonds?

BABE: No.

SZELL: Neither do I. *(Walking across the room carrying an electrical flex)* Not in today's market. Tomorrow I must go and find out before I go to the bank. *(He plugs the flex into in a socket on the wall to Babe's left)* You see…*(He walks back to the briefcase)* Your brother was incredibly strong. Strength is often inherited. He died in your arms. He travelled far and in great pain to do that. *(Behind the lid of the open briefcase, Szell plugs the other end of the flex into what sounds like a drill)* There has to be a reason.

BABE: *(Gasping)* I have no idea.

SZELL: *(Shouting to the door)* Karl!

(One of Janeway's henchmen enters. Babe, in panic, puts his head between his knees. The henchman pulls Babe's head back and his mouth open. Szell puts in a rubber bung to hold the teeth apart)

SZELL: *(Smiling)* Oh, please don't worry. I'm not going into that cavity. That nerve is already dying. A live, freshly cut nerve is infinitely more sensitive. *(He switches on the drill)* So, I'll just drill into a healthy tooth until I reach the pulp. Unless, of course, you can tell me that it's safe…

(Drill moves to camera, noise increases, picture blurs, Babe screams)

FILM
Marathon Man (1976)

DIRECTOR
John Schlesinger

STARRING
Dustin Hoffman, Laurence Olivier, Roy Scheider, William Devane, Marthe Keller

SCREENPLAY
William Goldman (from his own novel)

OSCAR NOMINATION
Best Supporting Actor (Laurence Olivier)

THE SCENE
Ageing Nazi Szell (Olivier) wants to inherit a fortune in diamonds stolen by his brother from Jews in prison camps during World War II. He hires corrupt secret agent Doc Levy (Scheider) to smuggle him from his hiding place in South America to New York where, working with intelligence chief Janeway (Devane), Szell visits a safety deposit box then kills Doc believing he planned to steal the diamonds from him. Next he and Janeaway capture his brother Babe (Hoffman), believing he knows about the heist. Szell ties Babe to a chair in a windowless room, tortures him with dental instruments and asks repeatedly and bafflingly: "Is it safe?". Later, Szell returns for a second session and this time performs his grim torture with an electric-powered instrument...

Miller's Crossing

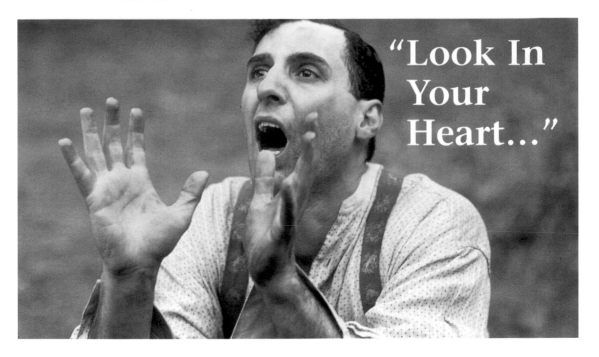

"Look In Your Heart..."

BERNIE: I-I-I'm just a grifter, huh, Tom? I-I'm, I'm a nobody. But I tell you what. I never crossed a friend, Tom. I *never* killed anybody, I never crossed a friend, nor *you*, I'll bet. *(Pointing to where the heavies are waiting)* We're not like those animals. This is not us!...This is a *dream*! *(Screaming)* It's a dream, Tommy I'm praying to you! I can't die! *(Sobbing)* I can't die! Out here in the woods...like a dumb animal! *In the woods like a dumb animal!*...Like a, like a dumb animal...I can't die...I can't die...I can't die out here in the woods like a dumb animal. I can't *(He falls to his knees)*...die! *(He bows, sobbing)* I'm praying to you! Look in your heart! I'm praying to you. Look in your heart. Look into your heart *(He repeats this like a chant. Tom raises the gun)*

I'm praying to you. Look in your heart. *(Tom takes aim)* Look in your heart. Look in your heart.

(Tom shoots, Bernie opens his eyes)

BERNIE: Tommy...

TOM: Shut up. You're dead. Get me?

BERNIE: I understand. I'm dead. God bless you.

FILM
Miller's Crossing (1990)

DIRECTOR
Joel Coen

WRITERS
Joel and Ethan Coen.

STARRING
Gabriel Byrne, Albert Finney, Marcia Gay Harden, John Turturro

THE SCENE
Tom (Gabriel Byrne) has been ordered by the mob boss to take double-crossing Bernie (John Turturro) for a one-way walk into the woods at Miller's Crossing...

TOM: Shut up. You have to disappear. You have to blow for good. No one can see you. No one can know.

BERNIE: God bless you.

TOM: Go somewhere no one knows you. Anyone sees you, you really *are* dead. I don't care. You're not my problem any more.

BERNIE: Of course not. Of course not. You've done your share. Thank you. Don't worry.

TOM: Shut up.

BERNIE: I understand.

TOM: Shut up.

BERNIE: Thank you.

TOM: Shut up. Just get out of here before I change my mind...

"Is There Or Is There Not, A Santa Claus?"

MARA: Your Honour, we request an immediate ruling from this court. Is there, or is there not, a Santa Claus ?

JUDGE HARPER: *(After a solemn pause)* Well...*(He is interrupted by the sound of his right-hand man, Charles Halloran, clearing his throat. Halloran points his cigar at the judge's office)* The court will take a short recess to consider the matter.

(Harper and Halloran repair to chambers, where Halloran informs the judge that if he rules against Santa, children won't hang up their stockings, stores will lose business, and no one will vote for him at the upcoming election. They re-enter the courtroom)

JUDGE HARPER: Before making a ruling,

this Court has consulted the highest authority available. The question of Santa Claus seems to be largely a matter of opinion. Many people firmly believe in him, others do not. The tradition of American justice demands a broad and unprejudiced view of such a controversial matter. This court therefore intends to...keep an open mind. We shall hear evidence on either side.

MARA: *(Turns to Mr Sawyer in disbelief)* He's crazy too! Your Honour, the burden of proof for this ridiculous contention clearly rests with my opponent. Can he produce any evidence to support his views ?

GAILEY: If Your Honour please, I can. Would Thomas Mara please take the stand.

MARA: Who, me?

GAILEY: Thomas Mara...Junior!

THOMAS MARA JNR: Hello Daddy! *(The ten-year-old lad walks past his astonished father)*

JUDGE HARPER: Tommy, you know the difference between telling the truth and telling a lie, don't you?

THOMAS: *(Earnestly)* Gosh, everybody knows you shouldn't tell a lie, 'specially in court. *(Everyone chuckles)*

JUDGE HARPER: Proceed, Mr. Gailey.

GAILEY: Do you believe in Santa Claus, Tommy?

THOMAS: Sure I do. He gave me a brand new flexible flyer sled last year, and this year –

GAILEY: And, er, what does he look like?

THOMAS: There he is, sitting there! *(Thomas stands up and points to Kris Kringle. The courtroom breaks into a further fit of polite chuckles)*

MARA: Your Honour, I protest!

JUDGE HARPER: Overruled!

GAILEY: Tell me, Tommy, why are you so sure there's a Santa Claus?

THOMAS: Because my Daddy told me so...Didn't you, Daddy?

(Mara nods reluctantly)

GAILEY: And you believe your Daddy, don't you Tommy? He's a very honest man.

THOMAS: Course he is! My Daddy wouldn't tell me anything that wasn't

so...would you Daddy?

(More laughter as Mara, by this point utterly defeated by his own son's honesty, shakes his head)

GAILEY: Thank you Tommy *(He lifts him back out of the witness box. Thomas returns to where his exasperated father is sitting)*

THOMAS: Goodbye Daddy!

(The courtroom guffaws again as he waves to his father and goes over to where Kris Kringle is sitting)

MARA: Your Honour –

THOMAS: *(Quietly to Kris Kringle)* Don't forget...a real official football helmet.

KRINGLE: Don't worry, Tommy. You'll get it. *(Tommy goes back to his mother)*

(Mara stares at his wife and son as Thomas, still grinning, waves to him once again. He turns to face Judge Harper)

MARA: *(Defeated, and with shame in his voice)* Your Honour, The State Of New York concedes the existence of Santa Claus...

FILM
Miracle On 34th Street (1947)
(entitled The Big Heart in the UK)

DIRECTOR
George Seaton

STARRING
Maureen O'Hara, John Payne, Edmund Gwenn, Natalie Wood, Gene Lockhart, Porter Hall, William Frawley

SCREENPLAY
George Seaton, Valentine Davies

OSCARS
George Seaton and Valentine Davies (Best Screenplay), Edmund Gwenn (Best Supporting Actor)

THE SCENE
Kris Kringle (Gwenn), who's been playing Santa at Macy's in New York, is attempting to convince everybody that he is the real Santa Claus. After attacking the in-store psychiatrist Mr. Sawyer (Hall), Kringle is confined to an asylum and looks certain to be committed. Unless, that is, lawyer Fred Gailey (Payne) can win a case against District Attorney Mr. Mara (Jerome Cowan) to the effect that Santa does indeed exist.

"Bring Out Your Dead!"

DEAD COLLECTOR: *(Trudging through plague-stricken village behind wooden cart piled high with corpses and pulled by a trio of emaciated, sackcloth-wearing wretches; he bangs a large triangle with a club)* Bring out your dead!

(Among the depraved sights in the village, we see an old crone beating a cat against the wall of her house. A couple wrestle in the mire. One old man seems to be climbing into a shopping basket in readiness for the Dead Collector)

DEAD COLLECTOR: Bring out your dead! *(A man dumps a corpse on the cart)* Ninepence. *(He pays up and walks away)* Bring out your dead!

LARGE MAN: *(Carrying an aged body over his shoulder)* Here's one.

DEAD COLLECTOR: Ninepence.

FILM
Monty Python And The Holy Grail (1975)

DIRECTORS
Terry Gilliam, Terry Jones

STARRING
Graham Chapman (King Arthur, various), John Cleese (Sir Lancelot, various) Terry Gilliam (Patsy, various), Eric Idle (Sir Robin, various), Terry Jones (Sir Bedevere, various), Michael Palin (Sir Galahad, various)

THE SCENE
England, 932 AD King Arthur (Chapman), son of Uther Pendragon, King of all Britons, Sovereign of all England, is recruiting a band of knights to join him in the court of Camelot. He's not getting very far. With lone servant Patsy (Gilliam) he passes through a typically disease-ridden, mud-caked village preceded by the Dead Collector (Idle), doing his rounds, collecting corpses at ninepence a go. Large Man (Cleese) attempts to get a not-quite-dead body (John Young) taken away...

BODY: I'm not dead.

DEAD COLLECTOR: What?

LARGE MAN: Nothing. There's your ninepence.

BODY: I'm not dead.

DEAD COLLECTOR: 'Ere. He says he's not dead.

LARGE MAN: Yes he is.

BODY: I'm not.

DEAD COLLECTOR: He isn't.

LARGE MAN: Well, he will be soon. He's very ill.

BODY: I'm getting better.

LARGE MAN: *(To Body)*: You're not. You'll be stone dead in a minute.

DEAD COLLECTOR: I can't take him like that. It's against regulations.

BODY: *(In child-like protestation)* I don't want to go on the cart!

LARGE MAN: Oh don't be such a baby!

DEAD COLLECTOR: I can't take him.

BODY: *(Wriggling)* I feel fine.

LARGE MAN: Do me a favour.

DEAD COLLECTOR: I can't.

LARGE MAN: Well, can you hang around a couple of minutes. He won't be long.

DEAD COLLECTOR: Nah, I gotta go to the Robinson's. They've lost nine today.

LARGE MAN: When's your next round?

DEAD COLLECTOR: Thursday.

BODY: I think I'll go for a walk.

LARGE MAN: You're not fooling anyone you know. (*To Dead Collector*) Look isn't there anything you could do?

BODY: (*Singing*) I feel happy, I feel happeee…

(*The Dead Collector looks around furtively. He clubs the old man on the head…*)

LARGE MAN: Ah, thanks very much

DEAD COLLECTOR: Not at all. See you Thursday.

(*King Arthur and servant Patsy, who is banging coconut shells together, "ride" past*)

LARGE MAN: Who's that then?

DEAD COLLECTOR: Dunno. Must be a king.

LARGE MAN: Why?

DEAD COLLECTOR: He hasn't got shit all over him …

"Done Her In"

MRS. HIGGINS: Hasn't it suddenly turned chilly?

LADY EYNSFORD-HILL: I do hope we won't have any unseasonable cold spells, they bring on so much influenza and the whole of our family is susceptible to it.

ELIZA: *(In a refined manner throughout)* My aunt died of it, so they said. But it is my belief that they done the old woman in.

LADY BOXINGTON: Done her in?

ELIZA: Yes, Lord love you. Why should she die of influenza when she'd come through diptheria right enough the year before? Fairly blue with it she was. They all thought she was dead, but my father, he kept ladling gin down her throat.

(Professor Higgins groans)

ELIZA: Then she come to so soon, she bit the bowl off the spoon.

LADY EYNSFORD-HILL: Dear me!

ELIZA: Now what call would a woman with that strength in her have to die of influenza? And what become of her new straw hat that should have come to me? Somebody pinched it, and what I say is, them as pinched it, done her in.

LORD BOXINGTON: Done her in? Done her in did you say?

LADY BOXINGTON: Whatever does it mean?

PROFESSOR HIGGINS: Ah, that's the new small talk. To do somebody in means to kill them.

LADY EYNSFORD-HILL: But you surely don't believe your aunt was killed?

ELIZA: Do I not! Them she lived with would have killed her for a hat pin, let alone a hat.

LADY EYNSFORD-HILL: But it can't have been right for your father to pour spirits down her throat like that. It might have killed her!

ELIZA: Not her. Gin was mother's milk to her. Besides, he poured so much down his own throat he knew the good of it.

LORD BOXINGTON: You don't mean that he drank?

ELIZA: Drank? My word, something chronic.

(Freddy laughs)

ELIZA: Dear, what *are* you sniggering at?

FREDDY: *(Plum firmly in gob)* It's the new small talk, you do it so awfully well.

ELIZA: Well, if I was doing it proper, what were you sniggering at? Have I said anything I oughtn't?

FILM
My Fair Lady (1964)

DIRECTOR
George Cukor

STARRING
Audrey Hepburn, Rex Harrison, Stanley Holloway, Wilfrid Hyde-White, Gladys Cooper

SCREENPLAY
Alan Jay Lerner (based on Alan Jay Lerner and Frederick Loewe's musical play and George Bernard Shaw's play Pygmalion)

OSCARS
Best Picture Director, Actor (Harrison), Cinematography, Art Direction/Set Decoration, Costume Design, Sound, Musical Adaptation

OSCAR NOMINATIONS
Best Supporting Actor (Holloway), Supporting Actress (Cooper), Adapted Screenplay, Film Editing

THE SCENE
Having bet fellow linguist Col. Pickering (Hyde White) that he can pass off Cockney flower girl Eliza Doolittle (Hepburn) as a princess via elocution lessons, Prof. Henry Higgins (Harrison) tests her progress by introducing her at the Ascot races. She has the accent to a tee though, sadly, not the refinement of language...

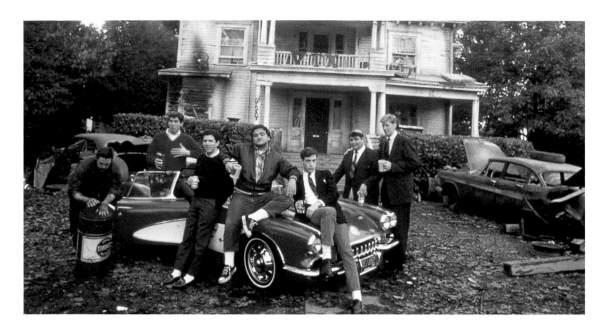

"Who's With Me?..."

OTTER: The war's over, man. Wormer dropped the big one.

BLUTO: What? *Over?* Did you say *over*? *Nothing* is over until *we* decide it is. Was it over when the Germans bombed Pearl Harbour? Hell no.

OTTER: Germans?

BOON: Forget it, he's rolling.

BLUTO: And it ain't over now, 'cause when the going gets tough...the tough get going. Who's with me? Let's go, come on, heeeyyy!...*(No one follows him as he charges out of the door. He skulks back in)*...What the *fuck* happened to the Delta that

I used to know? Where's the spirit? Where's the *guts*? Huh? This could be the greatest night of our lives, but you're gonna let it be the worst. *(Affects cowardly voice)* "Oh, we're afraid to go with you Bluto, we

FILM
National Lampoon's
Animal House (1978)

DIRECTOR
John Landis

STARRING
John Belushi, Tim Matheson,
Stephen Furst, Tom Hulce,
Peter Reiget, Donald Sutherland

SCREENPLAY
Harold Ramis, Douglas Kenney,
Chris Miller

THE SCENE
With the whole of Delta house
having finally been kicked out of
college, campus slob Bluto
(Belushi), backed by a stirring
classical score, rouses Otter
(Matheson), Boon (Reigert) and
the rest of the fraternity for one
final crazy act of revenge...

might get in trouble." Well just kiss my ass from now on. Not me, I'm not gonna take this. Wormer, he's a dead man; Marmalard, dead; Neidermeyer...

OTTER: Dead...Bluto's right. Psychotic, but absolutely right. We've gotta take these bastards. Now we could fight 'em with conventional weapons; that could take years and cost millions of lives. No, in this case I think we have to go all out. I think this situation absolutely requires a really futile and stupid gesture be done on somebody's part.

BLUTO: And we're just the guys to do it.

BOON: Let's do it!...

Network

"I'm Mad As Hell"

"We know the air is unfit to breathe, and our food is unfit to eat, and we sit watching our TVs while some local newscaster tells us that today we had 15 homicides and 63 violent crimes, as if that's the way it's supposed to be.

We know things are bad. Worse than bad. They're crazy. It's like everything everywhere is going crazy. So we don't go out any more. We sit in the house, and slowly the world we're living in is getting smaller, and all we say is 'Please, at least leave us alone in our living rooms. Let me have my toaster and my TV and my steel-belted radials, and I won't say anything, just leave us alone !' Well, I'm not going to leave you alone! I want you to get mad!

I don't know what to do about the depression and the inflation and the Russians and the crime in the street. All I know is that first you've got to get mad.

You've got to say 'I'm a human being, goddammit! My life has value!'

So I want you to get up now. I want all of you to get up out of your chairs. I want you to get up right now and go to the window, open it and stick your head out and yell 'I'm as mad as hell, and I'm not going to take this any more!'"

FILM
Network (1976)

STARRING
Peter Finch as Howard Beale, Faye Dunaway as Diana Christensen

WRITER
Paddy Chayefsky

DIRECTOR
Sidney Lumet

OSCARS
Best Actor (Finch, posthumously), Best Actress (Dunaway), Best Supporting Actress (Beatrice Straight), Best Screenplay

THE SCENE
Newsreader Howard Beale, having gone nuts on live TV, briefly rouses his viewers from their torpor...

"The Party Of The First Part..."

DRIFTWOOD:...Now pay particular attention to this first clause because it's most important. It says, "The party of the first part shall be known in this contract as the party of the first part". How do you like that? That's pretty neat, eh?

FIORELLO: No, it's no good.

DRIFTWOOD: What's the matter with it?

FIORELLO: I don't know, let's hear it again.

DRIFTWOOD: Says, "The party of the first part shall be known in this contract as the party of the first part."

FIORELLO: Sounds a little better this time.

DRIFTWOOD: Well it grows on ya – would you like to hear it once more?

FIORELLO: No, just the first part.

DRIFTWOOD: What do you mean? The party of the first part?

FIORELLO: No, the first part of the party of the first part.

DRIFTWOOD: All right, it says, "The first part of the party of the first part shall be known in this contract as the first part of the party of the first part..." Look,

why should we quarrel about a thing like this, we'll take it right out, huh?

FIORELLO: Yeah. It's too long anyhow. *(They rip off the top of the contract)* Now what have we got left?

DRIFTWOOD: Well I got about a foot and a half. Now it says, "The party of the second part shall be known in this contract as the party of the second part."

FIORELLO: Well, I don't know about that...

DRIFTWOOD: Now what's the matter?

FIORELLO: I don't like the

second party either.

DRIFTWOOD: Well, you should have come to the first party, we didn't get home till around four in the morning. I was *blind* for three days.

FIORELLO: Hey look, why can't the first part of the second party be the second part of the first party – then you got something!

DRIFTWOOD: Look, rather than go through all that again. What do you say?

FIORELLO: Fine. *(They rip off some more of the contract)*

DRIFTWOOD: Now I've got something here you're bound to like, you'll be crazy about it.

FIORELLO: No, I don't like it.

DRIFTWOOD: You don't like *what*?

FIORELLO: Whatever it is, I don't like it.

DRIFTWOOD: Well, don t let's break up an old friendship over a thing like that. Ready?

FIORELLO: Okay *(They rip off some more)* Now, the next part I don't think you're gonna like.

DRIFTWOOD: Well, your word's good enough for me. *(They both tear another clause off their contracts)*

FILM
A Night At The Opera (1935)

DIRECTOR
Sam Wood

STARRING
Groucho Marx, Chico Marx, Harpo Marx, Kitty Carlisle, Allan Jones, Siegfried Rumann, Margaret Dumont

SCREENPLAY
George Kaufman, Morrie Ryskind, Al Boasberg, Bert Kalmer, Harry Ruby

THE SCENE
In the Marx brothers' biggest and most extravagant hit, Manager Fiorello (Chico) and shyster Otis B. Driftwood (Groucho) are drafting a contract negotiating to bring "the greatest tenor in the world" to the New York Opera Company. After much shenanigans, they get down to the details...

Now then, is my word good enough for you?

FIORELLO: I should say not.

DRIFTWOOD: Well that takes out two more clauses. *(They rip out two more sections)* Now. "The party of the eighth part..."

FIORELLO: Naw, that's no good.

(They rip off another piece)

DRIFTWOOD: "The party of the ninth part..."

FIORELLO: Naw, that's no good. *(They rip off yet more. He compares the length of the contracts)* Hey, how is it my contract is skinnier than yours?

DRIFTWOOD: Well I don't know, you must have been out on the tail last night. But anyhow we're all set

now, aren't we?

FIORELLO: Oh yeah, sure.

DRIFTWOOD: Now just you put your name down there and the deal is legal. *(He hands Fiorello a pen)*

FIORELLO: I forgot to tell you *(handing it back)* I can't write.

DRIFTWOOD: Oh that's all right, there's no ink in the pen anyhow. But listen, it's a contract isn't it? We've got a contract no matter how small it is?

FIORELLO: Hey, wait, wait. What does this thing say here?

DRIFTWOOD: Oh that's the usual clause, that's in every contract, just says, "If any of the parties participating in this contract are shown not to be in their right mind, the entire agreement is automatically nullified."

FIORELLO: Well, I don't know...

DRIFTWOOD: It's all right. That's in every contract. That's what they call a sanity clause.

FIORELLO: Ha ha ha ha! You can't fool me, there ain't no Sanity Claus!

"I Coulda Been A Contender..."

"You remember that night in the Garden you came down to my dressing room and said 'Kid, this ain't your night. We're goin' for the price on Wilson'. You 'member that? 'This ain't your night'. My night! I coulda taken Wilson apart. So what happens? He gets the title shot outdoors in a ball park and what do I get? A one-way ticket to Palookaville.

You was my brother, Charlie. You shoulda looked out for me a little bit. You shoulda taken care of me just a little bit so I wouldn't have to take them dives for the short-end money...I coulda had class. I coulda been a contender. I coulda been somebody. Instead of a bum which is what I am, let's face it."

FILM
On The Waterfront (1954)

STARRING
Marlon Brando (Terry Malloy), Rod Steiger (as his brother Charlie)

WRITER
Budd Schulberg

DIRECTOR
Elia Kazan

OSCARS
Best Actor (Brando), Picture, Director, Screenplay, Supporting Actress (Eva Marie Saint), Art Direction, Editing, Cinematograpy

THE SCENE
Terry and Charlie's showdown in the back of the car...

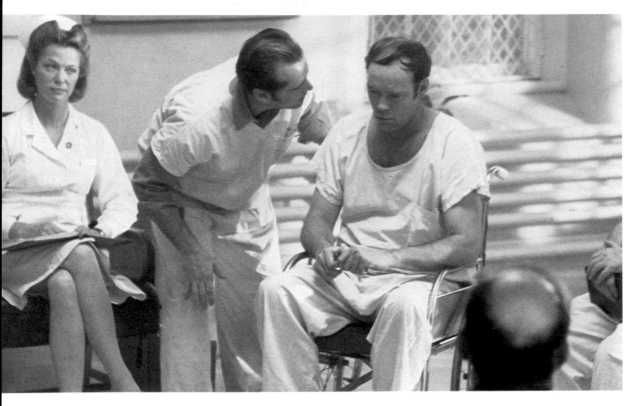

"No Crazier Than The Average Asshole..."

I'd like to know why none of the guys never told me that you, Miss Ratched, and the doctors could keep me here until you're good and ready to turn me loose. That's what I'd like to know. You heard me, Harding. You let me go on hasslin' Nurse Ratched here knowin' how much I had to lose, and you never told me nothin'. You can go home any time you want? You're bullshittin' me. He's bullshittin' me, right? Cheswick, you're voluntary? Scanlon? Billy, for chrissakes you *must* be committed, right? Oh...oh...gaw...I mean, you're just a young kid, what're you *doin'* here? You oughta be out in a convertible, why, birddoggin' chicks and bangin' beaver. What're you *doin'* here? For chrissake! What's funny about that? Jesus! I mean, you guys do nothing but complain about how you can't *stand* it in this place here and then you haven't got the *guts* just to walk *out*? I mean, what do you think you are for chrissake, *crazy* or somethin'? Well, you're not! You're not! You're no crazier than the average asshole out walkin' around on the streets and that's it. *Jesus Christ*, I can't even *believe* it!

FILM
One Flew Over The Cuckoo's Nest (1975)

STARRING
Jack Nicholson, Louise Fletcher

SCREENPLAY
Lauren Hauben from the book by Ken Kesey

DIRECTOR
Milos Forman

OSCARS
Best Picture, Best Script (Hauben), Best Actor (Nicholson), Best Actress (Fletcher), Best Director (Forman)

OSCAR NOMINATIONS
Best Cinematography, Best Music, Best Supporting Actor (Brad Dourif)

THE SCENE
Randall P. McMurphy (Jack Nicholson), having feigned lunacy in order to serve his prison sentence in the comparative comfort of a mental asylum, is appalled to learn that he won't automatically be released once his jail term is up...

"That's The Sign For Life..."

The Poseidon Adventure

(Beside a flooded chamber, Mrs. Rosen and husband Manny exchange glances)

MANNY: Val, be careful.

MRS. ROSEN: Manny, you think I'm planning to be careless?

(Adopts a series of extravagant diving-board postures and then takes an elegant plunge)

ROGO: What the hell does she think she's doing?

MANNY: Let her go – she *knows* what she's doing.

(Cuts between scenes of those in the dry waiting expectantly and Mrs. Rosen, swimming in the murky green waters. When she reaches Rev. Scott, she frees him and the others feel the rope go slack)

ROGO: *(Excitedly)* She found him. She must have found him!

MANNY: Oh, thank God!

(Cut to Mrs. Rosen dragging Hackman, their heads now

FILM:
The Poseidon Adventure (1972)

DIRECTOR
Ronald Neame

STARRING
Gene Hackman, Ernest Borgnine, Shelley Winters, Red Buttons, Carol Lynley

SCREENPLAY
Stirling Silliphant and Wendell Mayes

OSCARS
Best Song (The Morning After by Al Kasha and Joel Hirschhorn) Special Achievement Award for Visual Effects (L.B. Abbott and A.D. Flowers)

OSCAR NOMINATIONS
Best Supporting Actress (Shelley Winters), Cinematography (Harold E. Stine), Set Decoration (William Creber, Raphael Bretton), Costume Design (Paul Zastupnevich), Sound (Theodore Soderberg, Herman Lewis), Film Editing (Harold F. Kress), Original Dramatic Score (John Williams)

THE SCENE
New Year's Eve and the SS Poseidon, en route from New York to Athens, turns turtle when hit by a tidal wave caused by a seabed earthquake. After the boilers explode, flooding even more of the ship, a disparate group of survivors led by lay preacher Rev. Scott (Hackman) and an argumentative Rogo (Borgnine), makes its way through the upside-down vessel before being confronted by an underwater swim to escape, a desperate route which Rev. Scott must first ascertain is safe. As the seconds tick by without the promised signal of a tug on the rope he trails, Mrs. Rosen (Winters) volunteers to dive after him explaining that she is a former member of the Women's Swimming Association and that just because she hasn't put on a little weight lately doesn't mean she wasn't once an athlete...

above water. Reaching a girder, they cling to it. Cut to Rogo et al)

ROGO: They did it! They must have made it!

(Cut to Mrs. Rosen and Rev. Scott)

MRS. ROSEN: *(Still gasping)* You see Mr. Scott, in the water, I'm a very skinny lady.

(She begins to climb onto the girder but has a seizure and

falls back into the water. Rev. Scott dives back into the water and swims to her rescue. Cut back to Rogo et al)

MANNY: But there's no signal, they're not talking.

ROGO: Wait, wait! Give 'em time, will ya? Give 'em time!

(Cut back to Rev. Scott hauling Mrs. Rosen back to the girder where, in his arms, she gasps her final words)

MRS. ROSEN:
(Panting and in obvious discomfort) I guess I'm not a champion of the Women's Swimming Association any more.

REV. SCOTT: Hold on Mrs. Rosen, just hold on.

MRS. ROSEN: Enough is enough...

REV. SCOTT: No, no...

MRS. ROSEN: Let me go, please let me go. *(She fingers the medallion around her neck)* Give this to Manny. Tell him he has to give this to our grandson. For both of us. You see, that's the sign for life.

REV. SCOTT: Yes, yes...

MRS. ROSEN: Life always matters very much.

(She dies)

REV. SCOTT: Oh God, God not this woman, not this woman...

FILM
Psycho (1960)

DIRECTOR
Alfred Hitchcock

STARRING
Anthony Perkins, Janet Leigh,
Vera Miles, John Gavin

SCREENPLAY
Joseph Stefano (based on the
novel by Robert Bloch)

OSCAR NOMINATIONS
Director, Supporting Actress
(Leigh), Art Direction,
Cinematography

THE SCENE
Having finally been apprehended,
Norman Bates has at last
completely flipped and turned into
his mother. Sitting in the police
station wrapped in a blanket, he
talks to himself in her eerie voice
as the camera slowly moves
closer and closer. Describing how
she was forced into fingering
Norman for the murders at the
motel, Mrs Bates draws the movie
to a close...

"Why, She Wouldn't Even Harm A Fly..."

NORMAN: *(In His Mother's Voice)* It's sad...when a mother has to speak the words that condemn her own son. But I couldn't allow them to believe that I would commit murder! They'll put him away now, as I should have, years ago. He was always bad, and in the end he intended to tell them I killed those girls, and that man. As if I could do anything except just sit and stare, like one of his stuffed birds. They know I can't even move a finger, and I won't. I'll just sit here and be quiet, just in case they do...*suspect* me. They're probably watching me...Well, let them. Let them see what kind of a person I am. *(He looks down at a fly crawling on his hand)* I'm not even going to swat that fly...I hope they *are* watching. They'll see, they'll see and they'll know, and they'll say, "Why, she wouldn't even harm a fly..."

"I Don't Be Ticklin' Or Nothin'..."

FILM
Pulp Fiction (1994)

DIRECTOR
Quentin Tarantino

STARRING
John Travolta, Samuel L. Jackson, Uma Thurman, Harvey Keitel, Tim Roth, Bruce Willis

SCREENPLAY
Quentin Tarantino and Roger Avary

THE SCENE
Vincent Vega (Travolta) and Jules Winnfield (Jackson) arrive at a low-rent hacienda-style Hollywood apartment building. Taking the elevator route to a breakfast-time briefcase-repossessing encounter with some young enemies of gangster Marsellus Wallace, Jules tells Vincent of Marsellus' jealousy regarding his new wife Mia. He cites the time Marsellus had a couple of guys help the half-black half-Samoan Antwan "Tony Rocky Horror" Rockamora develop a speech impediment by throwing him off a fourth-storey balcony into a greenhouse – because Antwan gave Mia a foot massage...

(The elevator opens, Vincent and Jules – in white shirts, black suits and ties – exit and stride along the landing toward the apartment they seek)

VINCENT: But still I have to say, you play with matches, you get burned.

JULES: Whaddaya mean?

VINCENT: You don't be givin' Marsellus Wallace's new bride a foot massage.

JULES: You don't think he overreacted?

VINCENT: Well, Antwan probably didn't expect Marsellus to react the way he did, but he had to expect a reaction.

JULES: It was a foot massage, a foot massage is nothing. I give my mother a foot massage.

VINCENT: It's laying your hands in a familiar way on Marsellus' new wife. Is it...Is it as bad as eating her pussy out? No, but it's the same fuckin' ballpark.

JULES: Whoa...whoa...whoa...Stop right there. Eatin' a bitch out and givin' a bitch a foot massage ain't even the same fuckin' thing.

VINCENT: It's not, it's the same ballpark.

JULES: It ain't no *ballpark*, either. *(He stops and turns to face Vincent)* Now look, maybe your method of massage differs from mine, but touchin' his wife's feet and stickin' your tongue in the holiest of holies ain't the same ballpark – ain't the same league. It ain't even the same fuckin' sport. Foot massages don't mean shit.

VINCENT: Have you ever given a foot massage ?

JULES: *(Condescendingly)* Don't be tellin' me about foot massages. I'm the foot fuckin' master.

VINCENT: You given a lot of 'em?

JULES: Shit, yeah. I got my technique down and everything, man. I don't be ticklin' or nothin'.

VINCENT: *(Inching closer to Jules and lowering his voice)* Have you ever given a guy a foot massage?

(Jules looks at him long and hard, realising he's being wound up – and starts walking again)

JULES: Fuck you!

(Vincent, smiling, walks behind)

VINCENT: You given them a lot?

JULES: Fuck you!

VINCENT: You know, I'm kinda tired. I could use a foot massage myself.

JULES: Yo, yo, yo man, you best back off, I'm gittin' a little pissed here...

(Jules spots the number "49" on a door ahead of them)

JULES: This is the door...

"They Called Me Chicken"

JIM: Dad, I said it was a matter of honour, remember? They called me chicken. You know? Chicken? I had to go. Cause, I didn't I'd never be able to face those kids again. I got in one of those cars and Buzz, that...Buzz, one of those kids, he got in the other car and we had to drive fast and then jump, see, before the car came to the edge of the bluff and I got out okay and Buzz didn't and uh...it killed him. And I can't, I can't keep it to myself any more...That is *not* what I mean! Dad, I, I have never done anything right. I've been going around with my head in a sling for years! I didn't want to drag you into this but I can't help it. See, I think, I think that you can't just go around proving things and pretending like you're tough, and you can't...even though you got to...you look a certain way...*(Over his father's interjections)*...you can't...the look, that you feel...oh. YOU'RE NOT LISTENING TO ME! You're involved in this just like I am! Now I'm going to the police and I want to tell them I'm *involved* in this thing and I...*(Over his parents' objections)*...I DON'T KNOW! I don't know. It doesn't matter. It doesn't matter. It doesn't matter. It doesn't matter. It doesn't matter. It doesn't matter.

HIS FATHER: You can't be idealistic all your life.

JIM: Except, except, except! Except to yourself! Except to yourself. You don't want me to go. But I am involved! WE ARE ALL INVOLVED! Mom, a boy, a kid, was killed tonight! I don't see how I can get out of that by pretending that it didn't happen.

HIS FATHER: You know you did the wrong thing; that's the main thing.

JIM: That's nothing! That is absolutely nothing...Mom, I, just once I want to do something right! Dad, you better give me something. You better give me something fast...Dad, let me hear you answer her. Dad? Dad, stand up for me. STAND UP!

(He grabs his father, pulls him up and around and knocks him to the ground, choking him, then runs out...)

FILM
Rebel Without A Cause (1955)

STARRING
James Dean (Jim Stark), Natalie Wood (Judy), Sal Mineo (Plato)

SCREENPLAY
Stewart Stern. Adaption by Irving Shulman from a story by Nicholas Ray

OSCAR NOMINATIONS
Best Supporting Actress (Wood), Best Supporting Actor (Mineo), Best Motion Picture Story (Ray). (Dean also Best Actor nominee that year for East of Eden)

THE SCENE
After the schoolboy's test of courage has ended in death, Jim Stark (James Dean) appeals to his parents and becomes enraged by their concern that he should cover his own ass...

"Take 'Em To Missouri, Matt!"

FILM
Red River (1948)

STARRING
John Wayne as Thomas Dunson, Montgomery Clift as Matthew Garth

SCREENPLAY
Borden Chase and Charles Schnee from the Saturday Evening Post story by Borden Chase

DIRECTOR
Howard Hawks

OSCAR NOMINATIONS
Motion Picture Story (Chase), Film Editing (Christian Nyby)

THE SCENE
An epic cattle drive is about to hit the Chisholm Trail in 1865. Tough Texan cattle rancher Tom Dunson (Wayne) can't foresee the full extent of the dangers and drama ahead, but tries to warn the men he just can't stand quitters...

DUNSON: Well, we start tomorrow. We're going to Missouri with 10,000 head. Most of you men have come back to Texas from the War. You came back to nothing. You found your homes gone, your cattle scattered and your land stolen by carpetbaggers. Now there's no money and no work because there's no market for beef in the South. But there is in Missouri. So we're going to Missouri. Cumberland didn't make it. No one else has. That's the reason I'm here. I want you all to know what we're up against. You probably already know. But I want to make sure ya do. We got a thousand miles to go. 10 miles a day'll be good. 15'll be luck. It'll be dry country, dry wells when we get to 'em. It'll be wind, and rain. There's gonna be Indian territory, how bad I don't know. And when we get to Missouri there'll be border gangs. There's going to be a fight all the way, but we'll get there. Now, nobody has to come along. I'll still have a job for you when we get back. But remember this: every man who signs on for this drive agrees to finish it. There'll be no quitting along the way, not by me and not by you...*(In the dawn Dunson surveys the vast herd and assembled hands)* Ready, Matthew?

MATTHEW: All ready.

DUNSON: Take 'em to Missouri, Matt!

"Let's Go To Work..."

JOE: *(Pacing up and down, in no mood for laughing)* When this caper's over, and I'm sure it's gonna be a successful one, hell, we'll go down to the Hawaiian Islands and I'll roar and laugh with all of you. You'll find me a different character down there. Right now it's a matter of business. With the exception of Eddie and myself, who you already know, you're gonna be using aliases on this job. Under no circumstances do I want any one of you to relate to each other by your christian names. And I don't want any talk about yourself personally: that includes where you've been, your wife's name, where you might've done time, or a bank maybe you robbed in St. Petersburg. All I want you guys to talk about – if you have to – is what you're going to do. That should do it. Here are your names...Mr. Brown, Mr. White, Mr. Blonde, Mr. Blue, Mr. Orange and Mr. Pink.

(Mr. Pink looks disgruntled)

MR. PINK: Why am I Mr. Pink?

JOE: 'Cos you're a faggot, all right?

(The others burst into giggles, Messrs. Blonde and Brown most audibly)

MR. PINK: Why can't we pick our own colours?

JOE: *(Defiantly)* No way! No way! I tried that once, it don't work. You get four guys fighting over who's gonna be Mr. Black. They don't know anybody, so nobody backs down. No way. *(Stabbing his finger aggressively into his own chest)* I pick. You're Mr. Pink. Be thankful you're not Mr. Yellow.

MR. BROWN: Yeah, but Mr. Brown? That's a little too close to Mr. Shit.

MR. PINK: Mr. Pink sounds like Mr. Pussy. How about if I'm Mr. Purple? That sounds good to me, I'll be Mr. Purple.

JOE: *(Losing his patience)* You're not Mr. Purple. Some guy on some other job is Mr. Purple. You're Mr. Pink.

MR. WHITE: *(Turning to Mr. Pink)* Who cares what your name is?

MR. PINK: That's easy for you to say, you're Mr. White. You have a cool-sounding name. Now, look, if it's no big deal to be Mr. Pink, you wanna trade?

JOE:*(Exasperated)* Nobody's trading with anybody! This ain't a goddamn fuckin' city council meeting, y'know! Now, listen up, Mr. Pink...there's two ways you can go on this job: *(Points to himself)* my way or *(Points left)* the highway. Now what's it gonna be, Mr. Pink?

MR. PINK: Jesus Christ, Joe. Fuckin' forget about it. This is beneath me, you know. I'm Mr. Pink, let's move on.

JOE: I'll move on when I feel like it. All you guys got the goddamn message? I'm so goddamn mad hollerin' at you guys, I can hardly talk. *(Sniffs, significantly)* Let's go to work...

FILM
Reservoir Dogs (1992)

DIRECTOR
Quentin Tarantino

STARRING
Harvey Keitel (Mr. White), Michael Madsen (Mr. Blonde) Tim Roth (Mr. Orange), Steve Buscemi (Mr. Pink), Quentin Tarantino (Mr. Brown), Eddie Bunker (Mr. Blue), Lawrence Tierney (Joe), Chris Penn (Nice Guy Eddie)

THE SCENE
The final de-briefing before a bungled bank heist takes place in the same disused warehouse where, later Mr. Orange (Roth),will lie bleeding while Mr. Blonde (Madsen) cuts off the ear of a police hostage. Organiser Joe Cabot (Lawrence Tierney) is explaining to the six felons that they will adopt pseudonyms for the duration of the doomed "caper"...

"You Have My Permission To Withdraw..."

BRADLEY: *(Ushering the wildly swaying Princess Ann into his apartment, and muttering to himself)* I ought to have my head examined.

PRINCESS ANN: *(Sounding drunkenly confused)* Is this the elevator?

BRADLEY: It's my room.

PRINCESS ANN: *(Stumbling across the room)* I'm terribly sorry to mention it but the dizziness is getting worse. Can I sleep here?

BRADLEY: Well, that's the general idea.

PRINCESS ANN: Can I have a silk night-gown with rosebuds on it?

BRADLEY: I'm afraid you'll have to rough it tonight, in these.

(He hands her a pair of pyjamas)

PRINCESS ANN: *(Smiling brightly)* Pyjamas!

BRADLEY: Sorry honey, but I haven't worn a night-gown in years.

PRINCESS ANN: *(Regally)* Will you help me get undressed, please?

BRADLEY: *(Looking a tad taken aback)* Uh…Okay. *(He scans her from head to toe, then carefully undoes her necktie and hands it to her)* There you are. You can handle the rest.

(He crosses to the drinks cabinet, pours himself a glass of hooch and downs it rapidly)

PRINCESS ANN: May I have some?

BRADLEY: *(Firmly)* No. Now look –

PRINCESS ANN: This is very unusual. I've never been alone with a man before, even with my dress on *(She begins to unbutton her blouse)* With my dress off it's *most* unusual. I don't seem to mind. *(She gazes fondly at Bradley, who remains stony-faced)* Do you?

BRADLEY: I think I'll go out for a cup of coffee. You'd better get to sleep. *(Ann flops on to his bed)* No, no, no…*(He takes her arm and leads her towards the couch)* on this one.

PRINCESS ANN: How terribly nice.

BRADLEY: These are pyjamas. They're to sleep in. You're to climb into them, you understand?

FILM
Roman Holiday (1953)

DIRECTOR
William Wyler

STARRING
Audrey Hepburn, Gregory Peck, Eddie Albert, Hartley Power

SCREENPLAY
Ian McLellan Hunter, John Dighton

OSCARS
Audrey Hepburn (Best Actress), Ian McLellan Hunter (Best Motion Picture Story), Edith Head (Costume Design)

OSCAR NOMINATIONS
Best Picture, Director, Supporting Actor (Eddie Albert), Screenplay, Cinematography, Art Direction, Editing

THE SCENE
While on a goodwill tour of Europe, Princess Ann (Hepburn) feeling stifled by her schedule runs away from her royal lodgings, having been administered a sleep inducing wonder drug from her doctor to calm her frazzled state of mind. The effects quickly begin to show however, and when reporter Joe Bradley (Peck), who is unaware of her title, finds her in an apparently drunken state, he has no choice but to let her stay the night at his apartment…

PRINCESS ANN: Thank you.

BRADLEY: Then you do your sleeping on the couch, see. Not on the bed, not on the chair, on the couch. Is that clear?

PRINCESS ANN: *(Earnestly)* Do you know my favourite poem?

BRADLEY: You already recited that for me.

PRINCESS ANN: "Arethusa rose from her couch of snows in the Acroceraunian mountains" – Keats!

BRADLEY: Shelley.

PRINCESS ANN: Keats!

BRADLEY: Now you just keep your mind

off the poetry and on the pyjamas, everything'll be all right.

PRINCESS ANN: It's Keats.

BRADLEY: Now I'll be – it's Shelley – I'll be back in about ten minutes.

PRINCESS ANN: Keats.

(Bradley heads for the front door, pausing to put the bottle of wine out of Ann's reach on top of the mantelpiece. He then looks back at her, exasperated, before opening the front door)

PRINCESS ANN: *(Regally)* You have my permission to withdraw.

BRADLEY: Thank you very much…

"Sneeze And It's Goodbye Seattle!"

C.D.: All right, all right, 20 something betters. Uh, here goes. Uh, start with, uh, Obvious: Excuse me, is that your nose or did a bus park on your face? Meteorological: Everybody take cover! She's going to blow! Fashionable: You know, you could de-emphasize your nose if you wore something larger – like Wyoming. Personal: Well here we are – just the three of us. Punctual: All right Delman, your nose was on time, but you were 15 minutes late! Envious: Ooooh, I wish were you! Gosh! To be able to smell your own ear! Naughty: Uh, pardon me, sir, some of the ladies have asked if you wouldn't mind putting that thing away. Philosophical: You know, it's not the size of a nose that's important, it's what's in it that matters. Humorous: Laugh and the world laughs with you; sneeze and it's Goodbye Seattle! Commercial: Hi! I'm Ed Shive and I can paint that nose for $39.95. Polite: Uh, would you mind not bobbing your head? The orchestra keeps changing tempo.

Melodic, everybody: *(The crowd sings at his cue)* "He's got the whole world in his nose". Sympathetic: Awww, what happened, did your parents lose a bet with God? Complimentary: You must love the little birdies to give them this to perch on. Scientific: Hey, did that thing there influence the tides? Obscure: Huh! I'd hate to see the grindstone. Well, think about it. Inquiring: When you stop and smell the flowers, are they afraid? French: Say, zee pigs have refused to find any more truffles until you leave. Pornographic: Finally, a man who can satisfy two women at once. How many is that? *(He is answered – inaccurately – "14 chief!")* All right, all right! Religious: The Lord giveth, and he just kept on giving, didn't he? Disgusting: Say, who mows your nose hair? *(The crowd shouts "16!")* Uh, Paranoid: Keep that guy away from my cocaine! *("17!")* Aromatic: It must be wonderful to wake up in the morning and smell the coffee – in Brazil. *("18!")* Appreciative: Oooh, how original! Most people just have their teeth capped. *("19!")* All right, uh. All right. *(To boor)* Dirty: Your name wouldn't be Dick would it?

BOOR: You smart-ass sonofabitch.

C.D.: You flat-faced, flat-nosed flat-head. *(Turning his back, C.D. blocks a punch and thumps the dude without a glance.)* Has he fallen yet?

(Walks out to laughter and massive applause.)

FILM
Roxanne (1987)

STARRING
Steve Martin (C. D. Bales), Daryl Hannah (Roxanne)

DIRECTOR
Fred Schepisi

SCREENPLAY
Steve Martin

THE SCENE
A bar room boor unimaginatively insults C.D. Bales (Steve Martin) as "Big Nose", to which C.D. contends he can think of much better witticisms regarding his extraordinary proboscis. The number is established on a throw of darts...

"*That's* Gonna Be A Little Tough..."

PRIEST: You're willing to change for this woman?

BOYLE: For this woman, I'm willing to change. I mean, not just...I mean I would...if God gave me this woman, then there must be a God. So if He knows what's right, then I would do what's right by Him.

PRIEST: It's repent. Change your ways

BOYLE: *That's* gonna be a little tough. You know? I...

PRIEST: You love this woman, you will be willing to change.

BOYLE: Okay...I can still drink and take a few hits of a joint or something once in a while, all right? That's okay?

PRIEST: Twelve Our Fathers, ten Hail Marys, an Act Of Contrition.

BOYLE: That's it?

PRIEST: Ask the Lord for forgiveness...from your heart.

BOYLE: From my *heart*, huh. If I'd known this I would have come earlier, you know, before 33 years, you know?

PRIEST: You should have come earlier, yes.

BOYLE: I'll come back!

PRIEST: You follow in the way of Christ?

BOYLE: Uhhh...n-n-not *exactly*. I mean in my heart, yes, but...I've done a lot of...you know...kind of...you know carnal sins and a lot of, uh, drunk a lot of alcohol, and done some drugs. I've kind of weaseled around a lot in my life, you know, trying to get the edge all the time. But *basically* I would say that I'm a good-hearted person. I haven't really done anything *malicious* in my life. Um, I haven't done anything really very great in my life either. You know, tried to do some things, tried to find some truths. But I do love this woman. For her, I...

FILM
Salvador (1986)

DIRECTOR
Oliver Stone

WRITERS
Oliver Stone,
Richard Boyle

STARRING
James Woods, James Belushi, Michael Murphy, John Savage

OSCAR NOMINATIONS
Best Actor (Woods)
Best Original Screenplay

THE SCENE
Sleazeball journalist Richard Boyle, making a stab at redemption, goes to the cathedral in San Salvador to confess his many sins...

FILM
Schindler's List (1993)

DIRECTOR
Steven Spielberg

STARRING
Liam Neeson, Ben Kingsley,
Ralph Fiennes, Caroline Goodall,
Jonathan Sagalle

SCREENPLAY
Steve Zaillian

OSCARS
Best Picture, Best Director,
Best Adapted Screenplay,
Best Cinematography,
Best Original Score, Best Editing,
Best Art Direction

OSCAR NOMINATIONS
Best Actor (Liam Neeson), Best
Supporting Actor (Ralph Fiennes),
Best Costume Design, Best
Sound, Best Make-up

THE SCENE
Having maintained the safety of
over a thousand Jews by keeping
them as his workforce, Oskar
Schindler (Neeson) faces the
closure of the Plaszlow
concentration camp by the brutal
Nazi commandant Amon Goeth
(Fiennes), the surviving Jews
facing "resettlement" in Auschwitz.
Schindler's answer is to take as
many of them as possible to work
in his new factory and thus to
safety. Together with Jewish
friend, accountant Itzhak Stern
(Kingsley), he compiles the vital
list...

"The List Is An Absolute Good..."

After the long-winded and gruelling job of picking all those names that should be placed on the list of people to be transferred to Schindler's factory, Stern sits behind a desk concluding the work on a large black typewriter. Schindler paces the room restlessly, desperate to know how many more he can squeeze onto the list...

SCHINDLER: *(Urgent)* How many? How many?

STERN: 850, give or take...

SCHINDLER: *(Snapping)* Give or take what, Stern? Give or take what? Count them. How many?

(Stern begins counting hurriedly. We cut to moments later – Stern is still typing as Schindler, sitting nearby, peruses the list)

SCHINDLER: That's it, you can finish that page.

(Stern's typing halts)

STERN: What...did...Goeth say about this? You just told him how many people you need...(He pauses reading Schindler's face, stunned realisation entering his own) You're not buying them? You're buying them. You're paying for each of these names...*

SCHINDLER: If you were still working for me, I would expect you to talk me out of it. It's costing me a fortune.

(Still stunned, Stern busies himself with tidying the papers on the table in front of him)

SCHINDLER: Finish the page and leave one space at the bottom.

(Stern finishes and pulls the last sheet from the typewriter)

STERN: You...(He struggles to form the words. He lifts up the list and cradles it in his arm like a baby) The list is an absolute good. The list is life. All around its margins lies the gulf.*

The Shining

"Your Credit's Fine, Mr. Torrance..."

TORRANCE: I'd give anything for a drink. *(He sighs)* My god*damned* soul...just a glass of beer. *(He covers his face with his hands. Pulling them away his expression changes – a smile)* Hi Lloyd. It's slow tonight, isn't it? *(Laughs manically)*

BARTENDER: Yes it is, Mr. Torrance. What'll it be?

TORRANCE: I'm awfully glad you asked me that Lloyd, because I just happen to have two 20s and two 10s right here in my wallet. I was afraid they were going to be there next April! So here's what – you slip me a bottle of bourbon, a little glass and some ice. You can do that, can't you Lloyd? You're not too busy, are you? *(Laughs again)*

BARTENDER: No sir, not busy at all. *(He gets the bottle and a glass and places them in front of Torrance)*

TORRANCE: You set them up and I'll knock them back Lloyd, one b'one. White man's burden my man...white man's burden. *(He opens his wallet, peers into it and then looks up at the barman)* Say Lloyd, it seems I'm temporarily light. How's my credit in this joint anyway?

BARTENDER: Your credit's fine, Mr. Torrance.

TORRANCE: That's swell. I like you Lloyd. I always liked ya. You were always the best of 'em. The best goddamned bartender from Timbuktu to Portland, Maine...or Portland, Oregon, for that matter.

BARTENDER: Thank you for saying so.

(Jack drinks deeply, and stares into his glass, swishing the ice around)

TORRANCE: *(Suddenly)* I never laid a hand on him goddamnit. I didn't. I wouldn't touch one hair on his goddamned little head. I love the little sonofabitch! I'd do anything for him, any fucking thing for him. That *bitch*. As long as I live, she'll never let me forget what happened. *(He looks around conspiratorially before sighing)* I did hurt him once, okay? It was an accident...completely unintentional. Coulda happened to anybody. *(Shouting)* That was three goddamned years ago! The little fucker had thrown all my papers all over the floor – all I tried to do was pull him up...*(He pauses)* A momentary loss of muscular co-ordination. A few extra foot – pounds of energy per second per second...

(He snaps his fingers, shrugs and sighs. His reverie is then shattered by a shriek from the corridor outside...)

FILM
The Shining (1980)

DIRECTOR
Stanley Kubrick

STARRING
Jack Nicholson, Shelley Duvall, Danny Lloyd, Scatman Crothers

SCREENPLAY
Stanley Kubrick, Diane Johnson

THE SCENE
Jack Torrance (Nicholson) has taken his wife (Duvall) and his young son, Danny (Lloyd), to an isolated, snowbound Colorado hotel to perform caretaker duties while he writes his novel. As the weeks progress, however, Torrance begins to behave strangely and Danny has strange hallucinations – a tidal wave of blood engulfing a corridor and two mysterious twins appearing and disappearing. Then Danny encounters visions of a mind-bogglingly bloody massacre. When the boy runs to his mother with marks around his neck she assumes the former alcoholic Torrance has started drinking again and harmed his son. Enraged by the suggestion, Torrance wanders the hotel cursing and punching the air until he comes across the deserted ballroom where he approaches the bar and begins to talk to himself – or an apparitional barman Lloyd (Joseph Turkel)...

LECTER: *(Sniffing at the air-holes above him)* You use Evyan skin cream and sometimes you wear L'Air du Temps. *(He lowers his head and gazes at Clarice)* But not today.

CLARICE: *(Hastily changing the subject, noticing one of Lecter's works of art)* Did you do all these drawings, Doctor?

LECTER: Ah! That is the Duomo seen from the Belvedere. Do you know Florence?

CLARICE: *(Ignoring him)* All that detail just from memory, sir?

LECTER: Memory, Agent Starling, is what I have instead of a view.

CLARICE: Well, perhaps you'd care to lend us your view on this questionnaire, sir.

LECTER: Oh no, no, no, no! You were doing fine. You had been courteous, and receptive to courtesy. You had established trust with the embarrassing truth about Miggs. And now this ham-handed segue into your questionnaire. *(Tuts reproachfully)* It won't do.

CLARICE: I'm only asking you to look at this, Doctor. Either you will or you won't.

LECTER: Yeeeah. Jack Crawford must be very busy indeed if he is recruiting help from the student body. Busy hunting that no one Buffalo Bill. What a naughty boy he is. Do you know why he's called Buffalo Bill? Please tell me – the newspapers won't say.

CLARICE: Well, it started as a bad joke in Kansas City Homicide – they said, "This one likes to skin his humps."

LECTER: Why do you think he removes their skins, Agent Starling? *(Sarcastically)* Thrill me with your acumen.

CLARICE: It excites him. Most serial killers keep some sort of trophies from

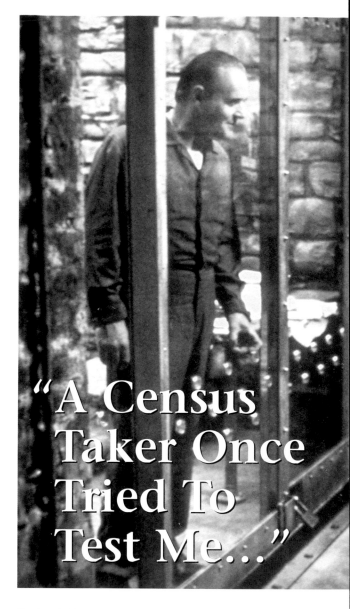

"A Census Taker Once Tried To Test Me..."

their victims.

LECTER: I didn't.

CLARICE: No. No. You ate yours.

LECTER: *(Indicating the questionnaire)* You send that through now.

(Clarice warily stands up and slides the questionnaire into Lecter's cell. He begins to thumb through it, smiling and winking at Clarice as he does so)

not more than one generation from poor white trash, are you Agent Starling? And that accent you've tried so desperately to shed – pure West Virginia. What does your father do? Is he a coal miner? Does he stink of the lamp? You know how quickly the boys found you. All those tedious sticky fumblings in the back seats of cars, while you could only dream of getting out, getting anywhere, getting all the way to the F...B...I.

CLARICE: You see a lot, Doctor. But are you strong enough to point that high-powered perception at yourself? What about it – why don't you look at yourself and write down what you see? Or maybe you're afraid to...

LECTER: *(Snaps the questionnaire back out of the cell)* A census taker once tried to test me. I ate his liver with some fava beans and a nice Chianti. *(He leans against the glass of the cell and lets loose a terrifyingly convincing slurping sound, as though he had just finished off a particularly piquant morsel of human flesh)* You fly back to school now, little Starling. *(Turns his back on her and, his voice dropping to a whisper)* Fly, fly, fly. Fly, fly, fly...

LECTER: Oh, Agent Starling, you think you can dissect me with this blunt little tool?

CLARICE: No! I thought that your knowledge –

LECTER: You're so ambitious, aren't you? You know what you look like to me, with your good bag and your cheap shoes? You look like a rube. A well-scrubbed, hustling rube, with a little taste. Good nutrition's given you some length of bone but you're

FILM
The Silence Of The Lambs (1990)

DIRECTOR
Jonathan Demme

STARRING
Jodie Foster, Anthony Hopkins, Scott Glenn

OSCARS
Best Picture, Best Actor (Hopkins), Best Actress (Foster), Best Director (Demme), Best Adapted Screenplay (Ted Tally)

OSCAR NOMINATIONS
Best Editing, Best Sound

THE SCENE
As part of a police effort to suss out the workings of serial killer Buffalo Bill's mind, rookie FBI Agent Clarice Starling (Foster) is assigned the task of interrogating Hannibal "The Cannibal" Lecter (Hopkins). Having extracted the information that she suffered verbal abuse from fellow prisoner Miggs (Stuart Levine) on the way in ("I can smell your c——" he hisses charmingly), the good Doctor turns the conversation towards fragrances of a less personal nature...

FILM
Some Like It Hot (1959)

DIRECTOR
Billy Wilder

STARRING
Tony Curtis, Jack Lemmon, Marilyn Monroe, George Raft, Pat O'Brien, Joe E. Brown

SCREENPLAY
Billy Wilder, I.A.L. Diamond

OSCAR NOMINATIONS
Best Actor (Jack Lemmon),Best Director, Best Screenplay, Cinematography (Charles Lang Jnr.), Art/Set Direction (Ted Haworth, Edward G. Boyle)

OSCARS
Costume Design (Orry-Kelly)

THE SCENE
Escaping from the Mob, Jerry/Daphne (Lemmon) tries to break off his engagement to Osgood Fielding III (Brown) with as much tact as possible…

"Well…Nobody's Perfect."

OSGOOD: I called mama. She was so happy, she *cried*. She wants you to have her wedding gown. It's white lace.

JERRY: Osgood, I can't get married in your mother's dress…She and I, we're not built the same way.

OSGOOD: We can have it altered.

JERRY: Oh no you don't. Osgood, I'm gonna level with you. We can't get married at all.

OSGOOD: Why not?

JERRY: Well, in the first place, I'm not a natural blonde.

OSGOOD: Doesn't matter!

JERRY: I smoke. I smoke all the time.

OSGOOD: I don't care.

JERRY: I have a terrible past. For three years now I've been living with a saxophone player.

OSGOOD: I forgive you.

JERRY: I can never have children.

OSGOOD: We can adopt some.

JERRY: *(Exasperated)* But you don't understand, Osgood! I'm a man!

OSGOOD: *(Entirely unfazed)* Well…nobody's perfect…

114

"Snails *And* Oysters..."

CRASSUS: *(Lying in his bath)* Fetch your stool Antoninus. *(Antoninus fetches the stool)* In here with it...This will do...Do you steal Antoninus?

ANTONINUS: *(He begins rubbing Crassus' back)* No master.

CRASSUS: Do you lie?

ANTONINUS: Not if I can avoid it.

CRASSUS: Have you ever dishonoured the Gods?

ANTONINUS: No master.

CRASSUS: Do you refrain from these vices out of respect for...moral virtues?

ANTONINUS: Yes master.

CRASSUS: *(After a long pause)* Do you eat oysters?

ANTONINUS: When I have them master.

CRASSUS: Do you eat snails?

ANTONINUS: No master.

CRASSUS: Do you consider the eating of oysters to be moral and the eating of snails to be immoral?

ANTONINUS: No master.

CRASSUS: Of course not...It is all a matter of taste.

ANTONINUS: Yes master.

CRASSUS: And taste is not the same as appetite, and therefore not a question of morals, is it? *(He begins to get out of the bath)*

ANTONINUS: It could be argued so master.

CRASSUS: My robe, Antoninus.*(Antoninus dresses him, Crassus gives him a sidelong glance).* My taste includes both snails *and* oysters...

FILM
Spartacus (1960)

DIRECTOR
Stanley Kubrick

STARRING
Kirk Douglas, Laurence Olivier, Tony Curtis, Jean Simmons, Charles Laughton, Peter Ustinov, John Gavin, Nina Foch, Herbert Lom, John Ireland.

SCREENPLAY
Dalton Trumbo (based on the novel by Howard Fast)

OSCARS
Best Supporting Actor (Peter Ustinov), Best Cinematography, Best Art Direction, Best Costume Design

OSCAR NOMINATIONS
Film Editing, Musical Score.

THE SCENE
Finding himself fiercely attracted to his handsome young slave Antoninus (Tony Curtis), Roman patrician Marcus Crassus (Laurence Olivier) tries to gauge the young man's sexual preferences. Though cut from the original cinema release by the censors because of the homosexual innuendo, the 1991 re-release featured a restored version of this scene. Because the original had been damaged, Anthony Hopkins redubbed the voice of the deceased Olivier...

"It's The Way They Think Of Me..."

GORDIE: Maybe you can go into the college courses with *me*?

CHRIS: That'll be the day.

GORDIE: Why not? You're smart enough.

CHRIS: They won't let me.

GORDIE: What do you mean?

CHRIS: It's the way people think of my family in this town. That's the way they think of me. It's the way they think of me. I'm just one of those low life *Chambers* kids.

GORDIE: That's not true.

CHRIS: *(Insistently)* Oh it *is*. No one even asked me if I took the milk money that time. I just got a three day vacation.

GORDIE: Did you take it?

CHRIS: *(Wearily)* Yeah, I took it. You knew I took it. Teddy knew I took it. Everyone knew I took it. Everyone knew it I think. Maybe I was sorry and I tried to give it back.

GORDIE: *(Surprised)* You tried to give it back?

CHRIS: Maybe. Just maybe. And maybe I took it to Old Lady Simons and told her and the money was all there, but I still got a three day vacation because it never showed up. Maybe the next week Old Lady Simons had this brand new sarong when she came to school.

FILM
Stand By Me (1986)

DIRECTOR
Rob Reiner

STARRING
Wil Wheaton, River Phoenix, Corey Feldman, Jerry O'Connell, Richard Dreyfuss, Kiefer Sutherland

SCREENPLAY
Raynold Gideon and Bruce A. Evans (based on the novella The Body by Stephen King)

OSCAR NOMINATIONS
Best Screenplay (Adapted)

THE SCENE
As they near the end of their odyssey to uncover the body of a missing schoolboy, 12-year-olds Chris Chambers (River Phoenix) and Gordie Lachance (Wil Wheaton) contemplate life by the campfire. Chris, the younger brother of Castle Rock bully "Eyeball" Chambers (Bradley Gregg), confides in Gordie his frustration at being labelled a black sheep...

GORDIE: *(Excitedly)* Yeah, yeah. It was brown and had dots on it.

CHRIS: Yeah, so let's just say that *I* stole the milk money but Old Lady Simons stole it back from me. Just suppose that I told the story. Me, Chris Chambers, kid brother to Eyeball Chambers. You think that anyone would have believed it?

GORDIE: No.

CHRIS: And do you think that that bitch would have dared try something like that if it had been one of those douchebags from up on The View, if they had taken the money?

GORDIE: No way.

CHRIS: Oh no. *(His voice cracks)* But with me I'm sure she had an eye on that skirt for a long time. Anyway she saw her chance and she took it. I was the stupid one for even trying to give it back. *(He starts to cry)* I just never thought...I never thought...that a teacher...Oh who gives a fuck anyway? It's just that I wish that I could go someplace where nobody knows me. *(Sobs)* I guess I'm just a pussy, huh...

"Gentlemen Of The Academy And Fellow Suckers..."

"Hey, that's fine! That's a very pretty speech, my dear, *very* pretty. You said the right thing. I want to be the very first one to congratulate you…on that…on that valuable little piece of bric-a-brac. Now *I* want to make a speech. Gentlemen of the Academy and fellow suckers…I got one of those once for a Best Performance. They don't mean a thing! People get 'em every year. What I want's a special award…something nobody else can get. I want a statue for the *Worst* Performance of the year. In fact, I want *three* statues for the three worst performances of the year because I've earned them. And every single one of you that saw those last masterpieces of mine *knows* that I've earned them. What I'm here to find out is, do I get 'em or do I get 'em. Now answer! Yes or no?"

(He flings his arm out, accidentally striking his wife a staggering blow…)

FILM
A Star is Born (1937)

STARRING
Janet Gaynor as Esther Blodgett/Vicki Lester
Fredric March as Norman Maine

WRITERS
Dorothy Parker, Alan Campbell, Robert Carson (Screenplay), William A. Wellman and Robert Carson (Story)

DIRECTOR
William A. Wellman

OSCAR
Writing – (Original Story) William A. Wellman and Robert Carson

OSCAR NOMINATIONS
Best Picture, Actor, Actress, Director, Screenplay

THE SCENE
The former film idol Norman Maine, on the skids and the booze, makes a pathetic entrance at the Academy Awards and interrupts his wife's acceptance speech as she clutches the Oscar for Best Actress…

FILM
Sunset Boulevard (1950)

STARRING
Gloria Swanson (Norma),
William Holden (Joe) and Erich
Von Stroheim (Max)

DIRECTOR
Billy Wilder

OSCARS
Story and Screenplay – Charles
Bracket, Billy Wilder and D.M.
Marshman, Jr.
Art Direction/Set Direction
(Black and White), Musical
Score – Franz Waxman

OSCAR NOMINATIONS
Best Picture, Actress
(Swanson), Actor (Holden),
Supporting Actor (Von
Stroheim), Supporting Actress
(Nancy Olson), Direction,
Cinematography, Editing

THE SCENE
Norma Desmond, star of
yesteryear, retreats into
madness after murder and
imagines that the newsreel
cameras are turning for her Big
Scene as Salome...

NORMA: What is the scene? Where am I?...Oh yes, yes. Down below they're waiting for the princess. I'm ready.

MAX: All right, cameras! Action!

(Norma descends the staircase to the music in her head and a voiceover from the dead Joe)

So they were turning after all, those cameras. Life, which can be strangely merciful, had taken pity on Norma Desmond. The dream she had clung to so desperately had enfolded her.

NORMA: I can't go on with the scene. I'm too happy. Mr DeMille, do you mind if I say a few words? Thank you. I just want to tell you all how happy I am to be back in the studio, making a picture again. You don't know how much I've missed all of you. And I promise you I'll never desert you again, because after Salome we'll make another picture, and another picture! You see, this is my life. It always will be. *(Her voice drops to a whisper)* There's nothing else...just us...and the cameras...and those wonderful people out there in the dark. All right, Mr DeMille. I'm ready for my close-up.

"Those Wonderful People Out There In The Dark..."

"You Talkin' To Me?"

Yeah. Huh? *(He pulls the gun)* Huh? Huh? Faster'n you.
Go fuck yourself. *(Puts the gun away)* I saw you comin'
you fuck, shitheel. I'm standin' here. You make the
move. *You* make the move. It's your move. *(Pulls the gun)*
Huh. Try it you...*(Puts the gun away)* You talkin' to me?
You talkin' to me? You talkin' to *me*?...Well who the hell
else are you talkin'...You talkin' to me?...Well I'm the
only one here...Who the fuck do you think *you're*
talking to? Oh yeah? Huh? Okay. *(Pulls the gun)* Huh?
(Voiceover begins) Listen you fuckers, you screwheads.
Here is a man who would not take it anymore, who
would *not* let...Listen you fuckers, you screwheads. Here
is a man who *would not* take it anymore, a man who
stood up against the scum...the dogs, the filth, the shit.
Here is someone who stood up. Here is...*(Pulls the gun)*
You're *dead*.

FILM
Taxi Driver (1976)

WRITER
Paul Schrader

DIRECTOR
Martin Scorsese

STARRING
Robert De Niro as Travis Bickle

OSCAR NOMINATIONS
Best Picture, Actor, Supporting
Actress (Jodie Foster), Original Score
(Bernard Herrmann)

THE SCENE
Frustrated loner Travis Bickle, taxi
driver, has flipped. In front of the
mirror in his squalid room he practices
drawing one of the guns he has
strapped to his arm under his army
jacket. He is muttering to himself and
addressing an invisible adversary...

"It Absolutely Will Not Stop..."

FILM
The Terminator (1984)

DIRECTOR
James Cameron

STARRING
Arnold Schwarzenegger, Linda Hamilton, Michael Biehn, Paul Winfield, Rick Rossovich, Lance Henriksen

SCREENPLAY
James Cameron, Gale Anne Hurd

THE SCENE
Los Angeles, 1984. Two time travellers seek Sarah Connor (Hamilton). The first traveller, the decidedly inhuman killing machine known as The Terminator (Schwarzenegger) aims to kill her. The second, nuclear holocaust survivor Kyle Reese (Biehn) is on a quest to save her life. After disposing of two other women called Sarah Connor in error, The Terminator tracks his real target to a night club, but Reese gets to her first. A lengthy car chase ensues as the pair attempt to escape their adversary. As they head for safety in an underground car park, Reese attempts to explain to the terrified Sarah just what is going on...

(The car, in its escape from The Terminator, screeches into the car park, sending the barrier flying)

REESE: *(Shouting)* All right, listen. The Terminator's an infiltration unit, part man, part machine. Underneath, it's a fully alloyed combat chassis – micro processor-controlled, fully armoured. Very tough. But outside, it's living, human tissue – flesh, skin, hair, blood, grown for the cyborgs.

SARAH: *(Hardly able to comprehend what she is hearing)* Look Reese, I don't know what you want from me –

REESE: Pay attention! Better ditch the car. *(The car screeches to a halt. He turns to face Sarah)* The 600 series had rubber skin. We spotted them easy. But these are new, they look human. Sweat, bad breath, everything. Very hard to spot. I had to wait till he moved on you before I could zero him –

SARAH: Look, I'm not stupid you know. They cannot make things like that yet!

REESE: Not yet, not for about 40 years.

SARAH: *(In disbelief)* Are you saying it's from the future?

REESE: One possible future. From your point of view; I don't know text stuff.

SARAH: Then you're from the future too, is that right?

REESE: Right.

SARAH: Right.

(She makes a grab for the door and attempts to escape from the car but Reese grabs her back again. There is a struggle, she bites his hand in a desperate effort to get away. He, in obvious pain, pulls her away and grabs her hands, while she is still struggling...)

REESE: *(Furious)* Cyborgs don't feel pain. I do. Don't do that again.

SARAH: *(In a tearful, pleading voice)* Just let me go.

REESE: Listen! Understand! That Terminator is out there! It can't be bargained with. It can't be reasoned with. It doesn't feel pity, or remorse, or fear. And it absolutely will not stop, ever, until you are dead...

Thelma And Louise

"Looks Like You've Got A Real Fucked-up Idea Of Fun..."

LOUISE: You let her go, you fuckin' asshole or I'm gonna splatter your ugly face over this nice car.

(Harlan faces her. Thelma lifts herself from the car bonnet, crying)

HARLAN: Alright...hey, hey. Just calm down. We're just havin' a little fun, that's all.

LOUISE: Looks like you've got a real fucked-up idea of fun.

THELMA: *(Sobbing)* Come on. Come on.

LOUISE: *(To Harlan)* Turn around...*(Harlan does so)* In the future, when a woman's cryin' like that, she isn't having any fun!

(Louise turns around and begins to head back toward her car)

HARLAN: Bitch! I should have gone ahead and fucked her.

LOUISE: *(Turning to look at him incredulously)* What did you say?

HARLAN: I said, "Suck my cock!"

(Without hesitation, Louise blasts him away. Harlan falls over the bonnet of the car. Louise shakily lowers the gun)

THELMA: Oh God! Oh my God!

LOUISE: Get the car!

THELMA: Oh Jesus Christ! Louise, you shot him. Oh-my-God!

(Thelma exits to find the car)

LOUISE: *(To Harlan's dead body, in exaggerated whisper)* You watch your mouth, buddy...

FILM
Thelma And Louise (1991)

DIRECTOR
Ridley Scott

STARRING
Susan Sarandon, Geena Davis, Harvey Keitel, Michael Madsen, Christopher McDonald, Brad Pitt

SCREENPLAY
Callie Khouri

OSCARS
Best Screenplay

OSCAR NOMINATIONS
Best Director (Ridley Scott), Best Actress (Susan Sarandon and Geena Davis), Best Editing, Best Cinematography

THE SCENE
Stopping at a roadside bar on the first night of their weekend spree, Thelma (Davis) is picked up by local redneck Harlan (Timothy Carhart) who forces himself upon her in the car park. Louise (Sarandon) arrives, just in time, and places the barrel of her gun on his neck...

"Watch The Skies!"

"All right, fellas, here's your story. North Pole, November third, Ned Scott reporting. One of the world's greatest battles was fought and won today by the human race. Here at the top of the world a handful of American soldiers and civilians met the first invasion from another planet. A man by the name of Noah once saved our world with an ark of wood. Here at the North Pole a few men performed a similar service with an arc of electricity. The flying saucer which landed here, and its pilot, have been destroyed, but not without casualties among our own meagre forces...I would like to bring to the microphone some of the men responsible for our success, but as Senior Air Force officer Captain Hendry is attending to demands over and above the call of duty...*(He turns to smile at Hendry, canoodling with a female crew member).* Doctor Carrington, the leader of the scientific expedition, is recovering from wounds received in the battle. And now, before giving you the details of the battle, I bring you a warning. Every one of you listening to my voice, tell the world. Tell this to everybody, wherever they are. Watch the skies, everywhere. Keep looking! Keep watching the skies!"

FILM
The Thing From Another World (1951)

DIRECTOR
Christian Nyby

STARRING
Kenneth Tobey, Margaret Sheridan, Robert Cornthwaite, Douglas Spencer, James Arness

SCREENPLAY
Charles Lederer

THE SCENE
At the end of this sci-fi horror paranoia favourite, reporter Scott (Douglas Spencer) radios a cautionary bulletin to the world's press from the North Pole...

"What Do You Believe In?"

"I still do believe in God, old man. I believe in God and mercy and all that, but the dead are happier dead. They don't miss much here, poor devils. What do you believe in?...Don't be so gloomy. After all, it's not that awful. Remember what the fella said. In Italy, for 30 years under the Borgias they had warfare, terror, murder and bloodshed, but they produced Michelangelo, Leonardo da Vinci and the Renaissance. In Switzerland, they had brotherly love. They had 500 years of democracy and peace, and what did that produce? The cuckoo clock. So long, Holly."

FILM
The Third Man (1949)

DIRECTOR
Carol Reed

STARRING
Joseph Cotton, Alida Valli, Orson Welles

SCREENPLAY
Graham Greene (from his novel)

OSCAR
Cinematography (Robert Krasker)

OSCAR NOMINATIONS
Direction, Editing

THE SCENE
Accused (rightly) of murdering children to make a fast buck with poisoned vaccine, Harry Lime, perhaps the smoothest villian in cinema, offers his infamously callous reply...

"One Louder..."

NIGEL: This is a top to a, you know, what we use on stage. But it's very, very special, because if you can see, the numbers all go to *11*. Look, *right* across the board. Eleven, 11, 11, 11...*(Nigel beams angelically)*

MARTY: Oh. And most amps go up to ten...

NIGEL: Exactly!

MARTY: Does that mean it's louder? Is that any louder?

NIGEL: Well, it's one louder, isn't it? It's not ten. You see, most blokes're gonna be playing at ten. You're on ten here, all the way up, all the way up, *all* the way up. You're on ten on your guitar. Where can you go from there? *Where?*

MARTY: I don't know.

FILM
This Is Spinal Tap (1982)

DIRECTOR
Rob Reiner

STARRING
Christopher Guest, Michael McKean, Harry Shearer, Rob Reiner

SCREENPLAY
Christopher Guest, Michael McKean, Harry Shearer, Rob Reiner

THE SCENE
Having given him the low-down on his guitar collection, legendary Tap plank spanker Nigel Tufnel (Guest) shows off his prized Marshall amp to bemused rockumentary film maker Marty Di Bergi (Reiner)...

NIGEL: Nowhere. *Exactly.* What *we* do is, if we need that extra push over the cliff, you know what we do?

MARTY: Put it up to 11.

NIGEL: Eleven. Exactly. *One* louder.

MARTY: Why don't you just make ten louder and make ten be the top number and make *that* a little louder?

NIGEL: *(Chewing his gum, drinking in the logic of the idea, dismissing it out of hand)* These go to 11...

"A Great Ape On A Football Field..."

FILM
This Sporting Life (1963)

DIRECTOR
Lindsay Anderson

STARRING
Richard Harris, Rachel Roberts, Alan Badel, William Hartnell, Colin Blakely, Vanda Godsell, Arthur Lowe

SCREENPLAY
David Storey (based upon his novel)

OSCAR NOMINATIONS
Richard Harris (Best Actor)
Rachel Roberts (Best Actress)

THE SCENE
Miner turned Rugby League pro Frank Machin (Richard Harris) is a violent boor, inarticulate but genuine in his feeling for his icy landlady Margaret Hammond (Rachel Roberts). In a rare reflective mood he expresses his need to his team-mate Maurice (Colin Blakely)...

FRANK: I don't understand her. I don't understand what she wants from me. "A great ape on a football field." That's what she called me. "A great ape on a football field." She makes me feel like that. She makes me feel clumsy. Awkward and big and – *stupid*. She makes me feel like, she makes me feel like I *crush*...*(he bangs his fists together)*...I *crush* everything. (*Some fans pass by, aiming some banter at Frank*) That's what *they* think of me, isn't it? A great ape on a football field. They want someone to act big, because they haven't got the guts to do it themselves. They want a hero and I am, I *am* a hero. But *she* won't admit it. Do you understand that? She *needs* me, Maurice, but she will *not* admit it. Maurice, I'm not going to be a footballer forever. I need something for good. Something *permanent*. Grab my hand. I *can* love someone, can't I? I can, can't I? I *can*...I need her. *(There are tears in his eyes)* She's the only thing that makes me feel wanted. I *can't* lose her...

FILM
Trainspotting (1996)

DIRECTOR
Danny Boyle

STARRING
Ewan McGregor, Ewan Bremner,
Robert Carlyle, Jonny Lee Miller,
Kevin McKidd, Kelly MacDonald

SCREENPLAY
John Hodge

OSCAR NOMINATION
Best Adapted Screenplay

THE SCENE
Having made several valiant but
failed attempts to kick his heroin
habit, Mark Renton (McGregor)
seems to have finally succeeded,
as have his mates Spud (Bremner)
and Sick Boy (Miller). However,
following a number of incidents,
notably a one-night stand with the
underage Diane (McDonald), who
resorts to a spot of blackmail in
order to keep Renton's attention,
the trio are soon sent spiralling
back into their old ways, spurred
on largely by the clean-living, drug-
free ways of Tommy (McKidd)
who takes them all on a fresh air
fuelled ramble…

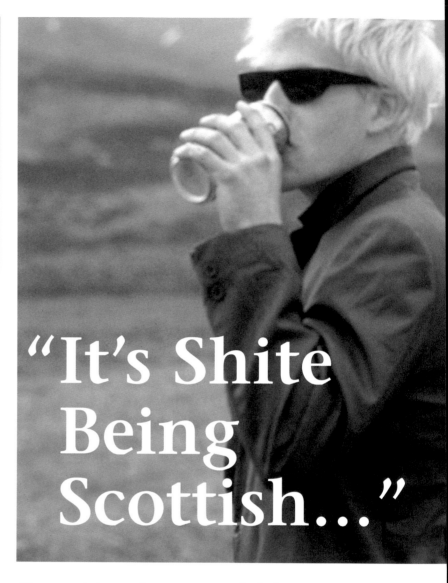

"It's Shite Being Scottish…"

(A train pulls up to a tiny station platform located for no obvious reason in the middle of a remote Caledonian moor. There are no discernible signs of life nearby. In the distance is a typically Scottish hill. As the train pulls away, Renton, Spud, Tommy and Sick Boy are left standing on the platform, dumbstruck by their surroundings)

SICK BOY: Now what?

TOMMY: We go for a walk.

SPUD: What?

TOMMY: A walk.

SPUD: But where?

(Tommy points vaguely toward the hill in the distance)

TOMMY: There.

SICK BOY: Are you serious?

(They all cross the railway tracks and Tommy begins his intended hill walking with gusto, but the other three fail to follow, opting instead to knock back a plentiful supply of booze. Tommy hasn't gone

very far before he realises he is alone, and turns to face the others)

TOMMY: Well, what are you waiting for?

SPUD: Tommy, this is not natural, man!

TOMMY: It's the great outdoors! It's fresh air!

SICK BOY: Look Tommy, we know you're getting a

hard time off Lizzy but there's really no need to take it out on us!

TOMMY: Doesn't it make you proud to be Scottish?

RENTON: *(Interrupting)* It's shite being Scottish! We're the lowest of the low, the scum of the fucking earth, the most wretched, miserable, servile, pathetic trash that was ever shat into civilisation! Some

people hate the English – I don't, they're just wankers. We, on the other hand, are colonised by wankers. We can't even find a decent culture to be colonised by. We're ruled by effete arseholes! It's a shite state of affairs to be in, Tommy, and all the fresh air in the world won't make any fucking difference!

(Renton stalks off. Sick Boy shrugs his shoulders and

follows suit, while a crestfallen Tommy gives up his hill walking quest and runs to catch up with Spud)

SPUD: *(Mumbling as usual)* I'm sorry, man.

RENTON: *(Voiceover)* At or around this time, Spud, Sick Boy and I made a healthy, informed, democratic decision to get back on heroin as soon as possible…

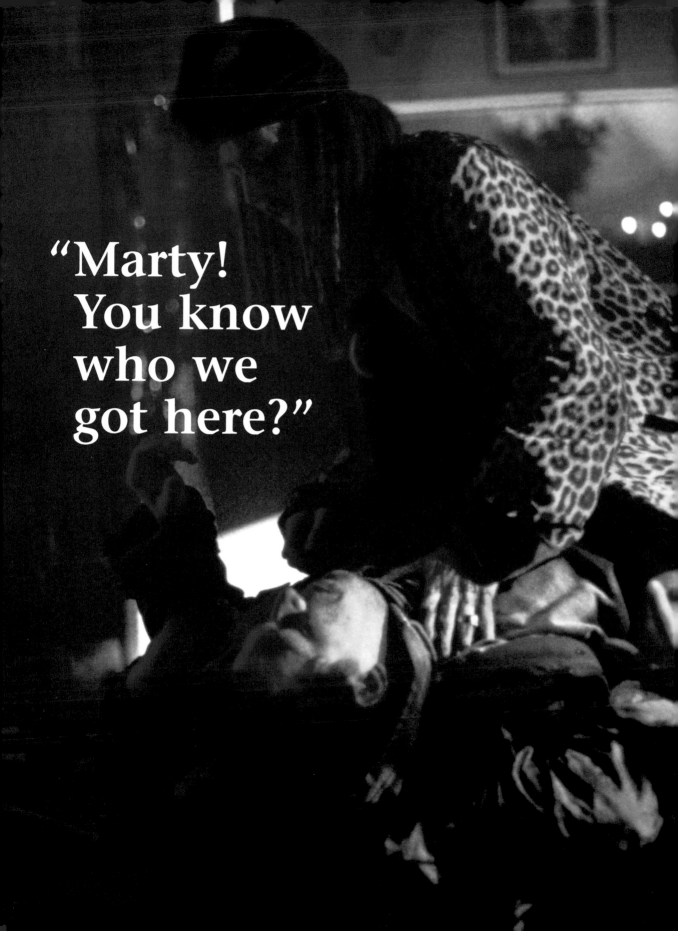

MARTY: *(Whispering to Drexl)* He was asking about Alabama.

DREXL: *(To Clarence)* Where the fuck is that bitch?

CLARENCE: She's with me.

DREXL: Who the fuck are you?

CLARENCE: I'm her husband.

DREXL: *(With a wry chuckle)* Well, that makes us practically related. Grab a seat, boy. Grab yourself a egg roll. We got everything here from diddle-eyed Joe to damned if I know.

CLARENCE: No thanks.

DREXL: *(Chuckling throatily)* No thanks? Wha' dat mean? I think you're too scared to be eatin'. *(Shines lamp in Clarence's face. He remains unmoved)* Let's see. We're sittin' down here, ready to negotiate. Hur. You've already given up your shit – I'm still a *mystery* to you. But I know exactly where your white ass is coming from. See if I asked you if you want some dinner and you grabbed the egg roll and start to chow down, I say to myself, "This motherfucker, he's carrying on like he ain't got a care in the world. And who knows? Maybe he don't. Maybe this fool's such a *baaaad* motherfucker he don't got to worry about nothin', he just sit down, watch my motherfuckin' TV." See? You ain't even sat down yet. And that TV over there, since you've been in the room there's a woman with her breasts hanging out. And you ain't even bothered to *look.* *(Clarence glances at the TV screen)* You just been clocking *me.* I know I'm pretty. But I ain't as pretty as a couple a titties *(Drexl swings the lamp towards Clarence, who catches it this time, glaring at Drexl, before hurling it back)* Ooh-wee! This job fits!!

(Drexl starts sniggering again as Clarence becomes increasingly moody)

CLARENCE: I'm not eating 'cause I'm not hungry. *(He places an envelope on the table)* I'm not sitting 'cause I'm not staying and I ain't looking at the movie 'cause I already seen it seven years ago. It's The Mack – Max Julien, Carol Speed and Richard Pryor. And I ain't scared of ya, I just don't like ya. In that envelope right there is some pay-off money, Alabama's movin' on to some greener pastures. We're not negotiating, I don't like to barter. What's in that envelope right there, it's for my peace of mind. My peace of mind's worth that much. Not one…Penny…More.

(Drexl rips open the envelope, looks inside and displays the contents to Marty)

DREXL: It's empty. *(Starts laughing maniacally again)* Marty! You know who we got here? Motherfuckin' Charlie Bronson! Mr. Majestyk. Looky here…Charlie. None of this bullshit is necessary. I don't got no hold over Alabama. I just tryin' to lend a girl a helping hand…

(He chucks the egg rolls at Clarence and takes a diving leap at the poor chap. There ensues ten minutes of gunplay, fisticuffs and swearing…)

FILM
True Romance (1993)

DIRECTOR
Tony Scott

SCREENPLAY
Quentin Tarantino

STARRING
Christian Slater, Patricia Arquette, Christopher Walken, Dennis Hopper, Gary Oldman, Brad Pitt, Val Kilmer, Bronson Pinchot

THE SCENE
Loner Clarence Worley (Christian Slater) has tied the knot with Alabama Whitman (Patricia Arquette), the kung-fu loving call-girl hired by his boss to make his birthday go with a bang. Before they can settle down to a life of wedded bliss, however, Clarence has the small problem of Alabama's sleazy pimp Drexl (Gary Oldman), whose brains he intends to blow out, after the ghost of Elvis (Val Kilmer) tells him it's the right thing to do…

"I'm Afraid, Dave..."

(Dave, clad in spacesuit and helmet, breathing heavily, heads across the galley towards the computer room, a look of murderous intent on his face)

HAL: *(In that chilling, whispery monotone)* Just what do you think you're doing, Dave?

(Dave ignores HAL's question and presses on)

HAL: Dave, I really think I'm entitled to an answer to that question. I know everything hasn't been quite right with me, but I can assure you quite confidently that it's going to be all right again. I feel much better

now. I really do.

(Dave begins disconnecting the back of the giant computer)

HAL: Look, Dave, I can see you're really upset about this. I honestly think you ought to sit down calmly, take a stress pill and think things over.

protests, floats weightlessly into the computer's internal workings)

HAL: I've still got the greatest enthusiasm and confidence in the mission, and I want to help you. Dave...stop. Stop, will you? Stop, Dave (*The monotone becomes slightly anxious*)...will you stop, Dave? Stop, Dave.

(*Dave floats further into HAL's workings*)

HAL: I'm afraid. I'm afraid, Dave. Dave, my mind is going. I can feel it. I can feel it. My mind is going. (*HAL's voice begins to slow down*) There is no question about it – I can feel it. I can feel it. I can feel it.

(*HAL's voice becomes slurred*)

HAL: I'm afraid. (*Changes tack very suddenly as Dave begins the shutdown process*) Good afternoon, gentlemen. I am a HAL

9000 computer. I became operational at the HAL plant in Irvana, Illinois on the 12th of January 1992. My instructor was Mr. Langley, and he taught me to sing a song.

(*HAL's voice becomes steadily slower and slower*)

HAL: Would you like to hear it?

DAVE: (*Breathlessly, in an almost comforting voice to the rapidly dying computer*) Yes. I'd like to hear it, HAL. Sing it for me.

HAL: It's called Daisy...

(*HAL breaks into song, ever slower, then grinding to a complete standstill at the end of the first verse. Dave, meanwhile, retracts from his disconnecting work and floats off...*)

(*Dave stubbornly removes the back of the computer*)

HAL: I know I've made some very poor decisions recently, but I can give you my complete assurance that my work will be back to normal.

(*Dave, ignoring HAL's*

FILM
2001: A Space Odyssey (1968)

DIRECTOR
Stanley Kubrick

STARRING
Keir Dullea, Gary Lockwood, William Sylvester, Daniel Richter, Leonard Rossiter, Margaret Tyzack

SCREENPLAY
Stanley Kubrick, Arthur C Clarke

OSCARS
Best Visual Effects (Stanley Kubrick)

OSCAR NOMINATIONS
Best Director (Stanley Kubrick), Best Original Screenplay And Story (Stanley Kubrick, Arthur C. Clarke), Best Art Direction (Tony Masters, Harry Lange, Ernie Archer)

THE SCENE
In the year 2001, astronauts David Bowman (Dullea) and Frank Poole (Lockwood) have enlisted the help of all-powerful computer HAL 9000 (the voice of Douglas Rain) to help them plot their course on a mission to Jupiter. After it becomes clear HAL (the three letters in the alphabet before IBM, geddit) is attempting to cover up a mistake by eradicating them, the pair secretly debate the possibilities of disconnecting him. Unknown to them though, HAL deduces their intentions via their lip movements, and takes his revenge by killing Frank in another "accident". Dave decides enough is enough, and heads for the technological rebel, disabling screwdriver in hand...

12 Angry Men

"Boy Oh Boy, There's Always One..."

JUROR ONE: *(Nervously)* Okay gentlemen, if I can have your attention...You fellas can handle this anyway you want to, I'm...I'm not going to make any rules. We can, well, discuss it first and then vote on it...Of course, that's, er, one way and, well, we can vote on it right now...

JUROR FOUR: *(Interrupting)* I think it is customary to take a preliminary vote.

JUROR SEVEN: *(Sarcastically)* Yeah, let's vote and get out of here...

JUROR ONE: Uh-huh... Okay then, I think that then...Of course, we have a first degree murder charge here and if we vote the accused guilty, ah, we've got to send him to the chair...That's mandatory.

JUROR FOUR: I think we know that.

JUROR TEN: Let's see who's where.

JUROR ONE: Is there anyone who doesn't want to vote?

(There is a hubbub of voices concurring. Juror Eight is noticeably silent)

JUROR 12: Fine with me.

JUROR ONE: Okay then, just remember this has to be 12 to zero either way, that's the law...Okay, are we ready? Now, all those voting guilty please raise your hands.

(Starting with Juror One, then Juror 12, hands are sporadically raised around the table)

JUROR ONE: One, two, three, four, five, six, seven – *(There is an abrupt pause)* eight, nine, ten, 11...Okay that's 11 guilty. Those voting not guilty.

(Juror Eight slowly raises his hand)

JUROR ONE: One. Thank you...Eleven guilty, one not guilty...Well, now we know

where we are.

JUROR TEN: Boy oh boy, there's always one.

FILM
12 Angry Men (1957)

DIRECTOR
Sidney Lumet

STARRING
Henry Fonda, Lee J. Cobb, Ed Begley, E.G. Marshall, Jack Warden, Martin Balsam, John Fielder, Jack Klugman, Edward Binns, Joseph Sweeney, George Voskovec, Robert Webber

SCREENPLAY
Reginald Rose (based on his teleplay)

OSCAR NOMINATIONS
Best Picture, Best Director, Best Screenplay

THE SCENE
After a long-winded court case, in which a Puerto Rican boy is accused of murdering his father, the jurors retire to gather in a sweltering New York court anteroom to debate the case. Stilted conversation, the opening of windows, general grumbling and wiping of sweaty brows – while one (Fonda) remains aloof – is followed by Juror One (Balsam) calling his fellow jurors to attention and gathering them around the central table. With continued irritation, the contrasting group of New Yorkers take their numerically ordered places – to his left Jurors Two (Fielder), Three (Cobb), Four (Marshall), Five (Klugman), Six (Binns), Seven (Warden), Eight (Fonda), Nine (Sweeney), Ten (Begley), 11 (Voskovec) and 12 (Webber) – to begin considering their verdict...

Unforgiven

FILM
Unforgiven (1992)

DIRECTOR
Clint Eastwood

STARRING
Clint Eastwood, Gene Hackman, Richard Harris, Morgan Freeman

SCREENPLAY
David Webb Peoples

THE SCENE
William Munny (Eastwood), an outlaw of "notoriously vicious and intemperate disposition", comes out of retirement to hunt down the cowboys who slashed a prostitute's face. Aided by The Schofield Kid (Jaimz Woolvett), a young and fearless outlaw, they ambush – and kill – the cowboys at their hold-up. The aftermath, however, leaves a very different impression for both of them…Munny and The Kid rest beneath a solitary tree, awaiting their reward money from the prostitutes. Munny stands, hat in hand, observing the trail ahead. The Kid, sat against the tree, drinks from a bottle of whisky to level his nerves…

"We All Have It Coming..."

KID: Say, Will?

MUNNY: Yeah?

KID: That was the first one.

MUNNY: First one what?

KID: *(Pause)* First one I ever killed.

MUNNY: Yeah?

KID: Know how I said I shot five men? It…it weren't true…ah, that Mexican who came at me with a knife? I just busted his leg with a shovel. I…I didn't kill him or nothing neither.

MUNNY: Well, you sure killed the hell out of that fella today.

KID: *(Tears forming)* Hell, yeah! *(He gulps from the bottle)* I killed the hell out him, didn't I? Three shots and he was takin' a shit!

MUNNY: Take a drink, kid.

KID: *(He talks another gulp, crying now)* Jesus Christ. It don't seem real. How he ain't never gonna breathe again. Ever. How he's dead. And the other one too. All on account of pullin' a trigger…

MUNNY: It's a hell of a thing, killing a man. You take away all he has and all he's gonna have.

KID: Yeah, well, I guess he had it coming.

MUNNY: We all have it coming, kid.

The Usual Suspects

"The Greatest Trick The Devil Ever Pulled..."

VERBAL: He's supposed to be Turkish. Some say his father was German. Nobody ever believed he was real. Nobody ever knew him or saw anyone who worked directly for him. But to hear Kobayashi tell it, anyone could have worked for Soze. You never knew. That was his power. The greatest trick the devil ever pulled was convincing the world he didn't exist...One story the guys told me – the story I believe, was from his days in Turkey – there was a gang of Hungarians that wanted their own mob. They realised that to be in power, they didn't need guns or money or even members, they just needed the will to do what the other guy wouldn't. After a while, they come into power and they go after Soze. He was small-time then – just running dope they say.

(Cut to a golden lit montage of a long-haired man entering a room to find his wife and three children being held at knifepoint)

VERBAL: They come to his home in the afternoon looking for his business. They find his wife and kids in the house and decide to wait for Soze. He comes home to find his wife raped and children screaming. The Hungarians knew Soze was tough, not to be trifled with, so they let him know they meant business. They tell him they want his territory, all his business.

(The first of the three Hungarians grabs Soze's only son and slits his throat)

VERBAL: Soze looks over the faces of his family then he shows these "men of will" what will really was.

(Soze aims his gun at the first Hungarian who is now holding a knife to his elder daughter's throat. Soze then points the gun at his wife and other daughter, shoots them without hesitation, then shoots his elder daughter and Hungarians one and two)

VERBAL: He tells him he would rather see his family dead than live another day after this. *(Soze motions to the one remaining mobster that he should leave)* He let the last Hungarian go, waits until his wife and kids are in the ground and then he goes after the rest of the mob. He kills their kids, he kills their wives, he kills their parents and their parents' friends. He burns down the houses they live in, the stores they work in. He kills the people that owe them money. And like that...*(He blows some imaginary jot from between his fingers)*...he's gone. Underground. Nobody's ever seen him since. He becomes a myth, a spook story that criminals tell their kids at night. "Rat on your pop and Keyser Soze will get you..." And no one ever really believed.

KUJAN: Do you believe in him, Verbal?

VERBAL: Keaton always said, "I don't believe in God but I'm afraid of him." Well I believe in God, and the only thing that scares me is Keyser Soze...

FILM
The Usual Suspects (1995)

DIRECTOR
Bryan Singer

STARRING
Kevin Spacey, Chazz Palminteri, Stephen Baldwin, Gabriel Byrne, Benicio Del Toro, Pete Postlethwaite

SCREENPLAY
Christopher McQuarrie

OSCARS
Best Supporting Actor (Kevin Spacey)

THE SCENE
Pulled in for questioning after a drugs deal turns into a bloody massacre, small-time hood Roger "Verbal" Kint (Spacey) narrates the story so far to cop Agent Kujan (Palminteri). Here he tells of the first time he heard the name of legendary super-criminal Keyser Soze...

134

The Untouchables

"What Are *You* Prepared To Do?"

MALONE: You said that you wanted to know how to get Capone. Do you really want to get him? You see what I'm saying? What are *you* prepared to do?

NESS: Everything within the law.

MALONE: And *then* what are you prepared to do? If you open the ball on these people, Mr. Ness, you must be prepared to go all the way, because they won't give up the fight until one of you is dead.

NESS: I want to get Capone. I don't know how to get him.

MALONE: You want to get Capone? I'll tell you what to do. He pulls a knife, you pull a gun. He sends one of your people to the hospital, you send one of his to the morgue. That's your tackle. That's how you get Capone. Now do you want that, are you *ready* to do that? I'm making you a deal. Do you want this deal?

NESS: I have sworn to put this man away with any and all legal means at my disposal, and I will do so.

MALONE: Well, the Lord hates a coward. *(They shake hands)* Do you know what a blood oath is, Mr. Ness?

NESS: Yes.

MALONE: Good, cause you just took one...

FILM
The Untouchables (1987)

DIRECTOR
Brian De Palma

STARRING
Sean Connery, Kevin Costner, Robert De Niro, Andy Garcia, Charles Martin Smith

SCREENPLAY
David Mamet

OSCAR NOMINATIONS
Art Direction/Set Decoration, Costume Design, Original Score

OSCAR
Best Supporting Actor (Sean Connery)

THE SCENE
Sickened by Al Capone's violent reign over prohibition Chicago, law enforcer Eliot Ness (Costner) agrees to meet veteran cop Jimmy Malone (Connery) secretly in a church to discuss getting rid of Capone once and for all. Malone chooses the occasion to give the young lad a tough lesson in life's realities...

136

"Greed Is Good..."

"Well, ladies and gentlemen, we're not here to indulge in fantasy, but in political and economic reality...I am not a destroyer of Companies. I am a *liberator* of them. The point is, ladies and gentlemen, that *greed*, for lack of a better word, is *good*. Greed is *right*. Greed works. Greed clarifies, cuts through and *captures* the *essence* of the evolutionary spirit. *Greed*, in all of its forms – greed for life, for money, for love, knowledge – has marked the upward surge of mankind and greed, you mark my words, will not only save Teldar Paper, but that other malfunctioning Corporation Galled the USA. Thank you very much. *(The audience rise to give him an ovation)* Thank you very much!..."

FILM
Wall Street (1987)

DIRECTOR
Oliver Stone

STARRING
Michael Douglas, Charlie Sheen, Daryl Hannah, Hal Holbrook, Martin Sheen, Terence Stamp

SCREENPLAY
Oliver Stone, Stanley Weiser

OSCAR
Best Actor (Michael Douglas)

THE SCENE
Gordon Gekko, the voice of the 80s, takes the floor at the annual shareholders' meeting of Teldar Paper, the latest corporation that he intends to take over and brutally strip of its assets...

When Harry Met Sally

HARRY: Why are you getting so upset? This is not about you.

SALLY: Yes it is. You are a human affront to all women and I am a woman.

HARRY: Hey. I don't feel great about it but I don't hear anyone complain.

SALLY: Of course not. You're out the door too fast.

HARRY: I think they have an okay time.

SALLY: How do you know?

HARRY: What do you mean 'how do I know'...I *know*.

SALLY: Because they...

HARRY: Yes, because they...

SALLY: How do you know that they are really...

HARRY: What are you saying? That they fake orgasm ?

SALLY: It's possible.

HARRY: Get outta here!

SALLY: Why? Most women at some time or another have faked it.

HARRY: Well, they haven't faked it with me.

SALLY: How do you know?

HARRY: Because I know.

SALLY: Oh right. That's right. I forgot. You're a man.

HARRY: What's that supposed to mean?

SALLY: Nothing. It's just that all men are

sure that it never happened to them and most women at one time or another have done it, so you do the math.

HARRY: You don't think I could tell the difference?

SALLY: No.

HARRY: Get outta here!

SALLY: *(Starting to run her hand through her hair)* Oooh. Oooh. Ooooooh!

"Oh God! Yes! Yes! Yes! Yes!"

HARRY: Are you okay?

SALLY: Oooooh. Oh God. Ooooh. Oh God! Ooooh. Aaaaah. Aaaaah. Oh God! Oh yeah, there, right there. Aaaaah. Oooooh. Aaaaaah. Oh God! Oh! Yes! Yes! Yes! YES! YES! YES! Aaaaaaah! Oh yes! YES! Oh! Oh! Oh! OH GOD! Oh.

(Smiles and returns to her lunch)

ELDERLY LADY: (*To Waiter)* I'll have what she's having.

FILM
When Harry Met Sally (1989)

STARRING
Billy Crystal as Harry Burns and Meg Ryan as Sally Arbright

DIRECTOR
Rob Reiner

SCREENPLAY
Nora Ephron

OSCAR NOMINATION
Best Original Screenplay (Nora Ephron)

THE SCENE
Ten years after their first meeting, Sally (Meg Ryan) and Harry's (Billy Crystal) friendship is still at the platonic stage. In a packed delicatessen, Sally challenges Harry over his irresponsible attitude towards women...

"You're Taking Me Illiterally..."

STAN: You know what? I think we've given that deed to the *wrong woman*. That's the first mistake we've made since that guy sold us the Brooklyn Bridge.

OLLIE: Oh, buying that bridge was no mistake. That's gonna be worth a lot of money to us someday!

STAN: Well, maybe you're right. We'd better go and get the deed.

OLLIE: Say! Maybe they won't give it back to us.

STAN: What do you mean they won't give it back to us? We'll get that deed, or I'll eat your *hat.*

OLLIE: That's what I call determination!

Some time later...

OLLIE: You said that if we didn't get the deed that you'd eat my hat.

STAN: Oh, now you're taking me illiterally.

OLLIE: Nevertheless, I'm going to teach you not to make rash promises. Eat the hat...

STAN: *(Crying)* I've never *eaten* a hat before.

(Bites, chews, gulps, cries... Considers the taste...Tucks a kerchief into his collar...Salts

the hat...Ollie snatches the hat back and furtively takes a nibble. Grimaces, spits it out and puts the chomped hat back on his head)

FILM
Way Out West (1937)

DIRECTOR
James W. Horne

WRITERS
Original story by Jack Jevne and Charles Rogers, Screenplay by Charles Rogers, Felix Adler and James Parrott

STARRING
Stan Laurel and Oliver Hardy

OSCAR NOMINATIONS
Best Score (Marvin Hatley)

THE SCENE
Stan and Ollie go through a laugh riot of song and sight gags as the prospectors entrusted with delivering the deed to a gold mine...

"There's No Place Like Home..."

FILM
The Wizard of Oz (1939)

STARRING
Judy Garland, Frank Morgan, Ray Bulger, Bert Lahr, Jack Haley

SCREENPLAY
Noel Langley, Florence Ryerson and Edgar Allan Woolf from the book by L Frank Baum

DIRECTOR
Victor Fleming

OSCARS
Special Award Judy Garland for Outstanding Performance as a Screen Juvenile, Best Song Over the Rainbow (Music by Harold Arlen, lyrics by E.V. Harburg), Best Original Score Herbert Stothart

OSCAR NOMINATIONS
Best Picture, Art Direction, Special Effects

THE SCENE
After her strange and terrible adventures in Oz, Dorothy (Judy Garland) learns the secret of the ruby slippers and returns to Kansas. Waking in her own bed she finds herself surrounded by old friends who think she's had a dream...

TIN MAN: What have you learned, Dorothy?

DOROTHY: Well...I think that it, that it wasn't enough just to want to see Uncle Henry and Auntie Em. And it's that if I ever go looking for my heart's desire again I won't look any further than my own back yard. Because if it isn't there I never really lost it to begin with. Is that right? *(Shuts her eyes and clicks her heels together.)* There's no place like home. There's no place like home. There's no place like home...Oh Auntie Em, it's you! But I did leave you, Uncle Henry. That's just the trouble. And I tried to get back for days and days...But it wasn't a dream. It was a place. And you, and you, and you...and you were *there*. But you couldn't have been, could you?...No, Aunt Em, this was a real, truly, live place. And I remember that some if it wasn't very nice. But most of it was *beautiful*. But just the same all I kept saying to everybody was I want to go home. And they sent me home. Doesn't anybody believe me? Oh but anyway, Toto, we're home. Home! And this is my room. And you're all here. And I'm not gonna leave here ever, ever again, Because I love you all, and, oh Auntie Em, there's no place like home!

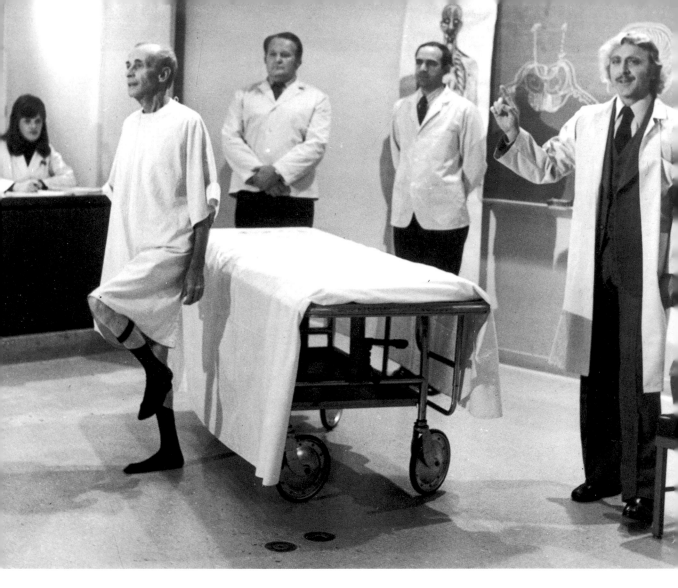

"That's Frun-Ken-Steeeen..."

FRANKENSTEIN: Are there any more questions before we proceed?

MEDICAL STUDENT: I have one question, Dr. Frankenstein.

FRANKENSTEIN: (*Turns to face the class with a face like thunder*) That's *Frun-ken-steeeen.*

MEDICAL STUDENT:

(*Takes his glasses off in apparent surprise*) I beg your pardon?

FRANKENSTEIN: My name. It's pronounced Frun-ken-steeeen.

MEDICAL STUDENT: But aren't you the grandson of the famous Dr. Victor Frankenstein who went into graveyards, dug up freshly buried corpses, and

transformed dead components into –

FRANKENSTEIN: Yes, yes, yes! (*With much embarrassed mirth*) We all know what he did. (*Nervous chuckles among the students*) But I'd rather be remembered for my own small contributions to science (*he guiltily rinses his fingers in the bowl of water on his desk*), and not because of my accidental relationship to a famous... cuckoo! *(Laughter)*. Now if you don't mind, can we get on with your question...

(There follows a lengthy explanation of the distinction between reflexive and voluntary nerve impulses, involving Dr. Frankenstein dealing out much physical abuse to an unfortunate old man called Mr. Hilltop. At the end of it...)

FRANKENSTEIN: Are there any last questions before we leave?

MEDICAL STUDENT: *(Stands up)* Dr. Frank – *(The Dr. stares at him in annoyance)* Dr. Frun-ken-steeeen.

FRANKENSTEIN: Yes?

MEDICAL STUDENT: Isn't it true that Darwin preserved a piece of vermicelli in a glass case until, by some extraordinary means, it actually began to move with a voluntary motion?

FRANKENSTEIN: *(Sarcastically)* Are you speaking of the worm or the spaghetti?

MEDICAL STUDENT: Why, the worm, sir.

FRANKENSTEIN: Yes. It seems to me I did read something of that incident when I was a student, *(sits down by his desk)* but *(adopting a smug tone)* you

have to remember that a worm, with very few exceptions, is not a human being. *(Laughter)*

MEDICAL STUDENT: But wasn't that the whole basis of your grandfather's work, sir? The re-animation of dead tissue?

FRANKENSTEIN: *(Mutters crossly)* My grandfather was a very sick man.

MEDICAL STUDENT: But as a Frankenstein, aren't you the least bit curious about it? Doesn't the bringing back to life of what was once dead hold any intrigue for you?

(Herr Falkstein begins to listen carefully to the ensuing debate)

FILM
Young Frankenstein (1974)

DIRECTOR
Mel Brooks

SCREENPLAY
Gene Wilder. Mel Brooks

STARRING
Gene Wilder, Marty Feldman, Madeline Kahn, Peter Boyle, Cloris Leachman, Teri Garr, Gene Hackman

THE SCENE
Dr. Frederick Frankenstein (Gene Wilder), scientist and grandson of the legendary Dr. Victor Frankenstein, the man who became famous bringing the dead back to life, is explaining the workings of the human brain to his class of attentive students, unaware that the details of his great grandfather's will have been slipped into the classroom along with Herr Falkstein (Richard Hadyn), a family friend. Unfortunately, one of the Doctor's students chooses that moment to get inquisitive about Frankenstein family matters, a touchy subject at the best of times...

FRANKENSTEIN: *(Getting worked up)* You are talking about the nonsensical ravings of a lunatic mind. Dead is dead!

MEDICAL STUDENT: But look at what has been done with hearts and kidneys!

FRANKENSTEIN: Hearts and kidneys are tinker toys! I'm talking about the central nervous system!

MEDICAL STUDENT: But sir...

FRANKENSTEIN: *(Hopping mad)* I am a scientist, not a philosopher! You have more chance of *(he picks a scalpel off the desk)* re-animating this scalpel than of mending a broken nervous system!

MEDICAL STUDENT: But what about your grandfather's work, sir?

FRANKENSTEIN: *(Completely losing his rag)* My grandfather's work was doo-doo! *(Much consternation and gasping among the students while Herr Falkstein almost alarmed by the Doctor's behaviour)* I am not interested in death! The only thing that concerns me is the preservation of life! *(In saying so, he rams the scalpel into his thigh. Realising what he's done, he crosses his legs, and in a pained voice)* Class...is... dismissed...

The Abyss
(20th Century Fox)

Alfie
(British Film Institute/Paramount)

Alien
(Kobal)

All The President's Men
(Warner Bros)

The Apartment
(British Film Institute/ MGM)

Apocalypse Now
(Pictorial Press)

Basic Instinct
(Pictorial Press)

The Big Lebowski
(Moviestore/ Polygram)

The Big Sleep
(Pictorial Press)

Blade Runner
(Moviestore/ The Ladd Company/ The Blade Runner Partnership)

Brief Encounter
(British Film Institute/ Carlton)

Bringing Up Baby
(British Film Institute/ RKO Radio Pictures Inc.)

Bull Durham
(British Film Institute/ MGM)

Bus Stop
(British Film Institute/ 20th Century Fox)

Butch Cassidy And The Sundance Kid
(Ronald Grant)

Casablanca
(Turner Entertainment Co.)

The Crying Game
(Pictorial Press)

Dead Poets Society
(Touchstone)

The Deer Hunter
(British Film Institute/EMI)

Diner
(Moviestore/ Turner Entertainment Co.)

Dirty Harry
(Moviestore/ Warner Bros./ The Malapso Co.)

Dr No
(Moviestore/ Don Jaq and United Artists)

Everything You Always Wanted To Know About Sex, But Were Afraid To Ask
(United Artists/ MGM)

Fatal Attraction
(Pictorial Press)

A Few Good Men
(Castle Rock Entertainment)

A Fistful Of Dollars
(Ronald Grant)

Five Easy Pieces
(Columbia Pictures)

The Fly
(Moviestore/ 20th Century Fox)

42nd Street
(Moviestore/ Warner Bros)

Full Metal Jacket
(Pictorial Press)

Glengarry Glen Ross
(British Film Institute/New Line)

The Godfather
(Ronald Grant)

Gone With The Wind
(Ronald Grant)

Good Morning Vietnam
(Pictorial Press)

Good Will Hunting
(Moviestore/ Laurence Bendier Productions)

Goodfellas
(Moviestore/ Warner Bros)

The Graduate
(Pictorial Press)

The Grapes Of Wrath
(British Film Institute/ 20th Century Fox)

Gremlins
(Pictorial Press)

A Hard Day's Night
(British Film Institute/ United Artists)

Heat
(Moviestore/ Monarchy Ent. & Regency Ent.)

The Hustler
(Pictorial Press)

In The Name Of The Father
(Pictorial Press)

In Which We Serve
(British Film Institute/Carlton)

The Incredible Shrinking Man
(Scope Features)

It's A Wonderful Life
(British Film Institute/ Polygram)

The Italian Job
(Moviestore/ Paramount)

Jaws
(Pictorial Press)

The Jungle Book
(Pictorial Press)

LA Confidential
(Kobal)

Local Hero
(British Film Institute/ Celandine Films)

The Long Good Friday
(Handmade Films)

Manhattan
(Pictorial Press)

Marathon Man
(British Film Institute/ Paramount)

Miller's Crossing
(Ronald Grant)

Miracle on 34th Street
(British Film Institute/ 20th Century Fox)

Monty Python & The Holy Grail
(British Film Institute/ National Film Trustee Co.)

My Fair Lady
(Moviestore/ Warner Bros)

National Lampoon's Animal House
(British Film Institute/ University City Studios Inc.)

Network
(Aquarius)

Night At The Opera
(Kobal)

On The Waterfront
(Pictorial Press)

One Flew Over The Cuckoo's Nest
(Pictorial Press)

The Poseidon Adventure
(British Film Institute/20th Century Fox)

Psycho
(Moviestore/ Shanley Production Inc.)

Pulp Fiction
(Miramax)

Rebel Without A Cause
(London Features)

Red River
(British Film Institute/ MGM/ United Artists)

Reservoir Dogs
(Pictorial Press)

Roman Holiday
(British Film Institute)

Roxanne
(Moviestore/ Columbia Pictures)

Salvador
(Moviestore/ Hemdale Film Corporation)

Schindler's List
(Pictorial Press)

The Shining
(Pictorial Press)

The Silence Of The Lambs
(British Film Institute/ Orion)

Some Like It Hot
(Moviestore/ MGM)

Spartacus
(Universal)

Stand By Me
(Moviestore/ Columbia Pictures)

A Star Is Born
(British Film Institute/ Warner Bros)

Sunset Boulevard
(Pictorial Press)

Taxi Driver
(Pictorial Press)

The Terminator
(Pictorial Press)

Thelma And Louise
(MGM)

The Thing From Another World
(British Film Institute/ University City Studios Inc.)

This Is Spinal Tap
(Moviestore/ Embassy Pictures)

The Third Man
(Pictorial Press)

This Sporting Life
(British Film Institute/Carlton)

Trainspotting
(Pictorial Press)

True Romance
(August Entertainment Inc)

12 Angry Men
(British Film Institute/ Orion)

2001: A Space Odyssey
(British Film Institute/MGM)

Unforgiven
(Ronald Grant)

The Untouchables
(Pictorial Press)

The Usual Suspects
(Pictorial Press)

Wall Street
(Moviestore/ Fox)

Way Out West
(Ronald Grant)

When Harry Met Sally
(Pictorial Press)

The Wizard of Oz
(British Film Institute/ Turner Entertainment Co.)

Young Frankenstein
(Ronald Grant)